$\mathcal{A}$

WICKED
GOOD IDEA

Written by:

Tracey Noonan,

Dani Vilagie, and

the Wicked Good Cupcake Family

REVIEWS

"When I called my dad and asked him how to start a cake business, he said, 'sell a cake.' Best advice I ever got. Now when people ask me how to start a business, I can say, 'sell something and read **A Wicked Good Idea.**' There's a million ways to become an entrepreneur and a billion mistakes to make. Tracey Noonan takes you on that journey with all its ups and downs. **A Wicked Good Idea** is an inspirational journey by a team who has walked the path and lived to tell the tale." **Chef Duff Goldman, Owner of Charm City Cakes,** http://www.charmcitycakes.com/.

"Not afraid to power through, push on, and overcome obstacles thrown in her path, Tracy Noonan embodies true entrepreneurial spirit.

With a novel idea, grit, determination and tenacity, she has achieved the American dream.

An inspiration to those willing to put in the time and do the work, **A Wicked Good Idea** is a roadmap for all seeking entrepreneurial success. A must read." **Laine Raia- Author/Editor and Proprietor of The Ponderaia,** www.ponderaia.com **North Reading, MA.**

"In this delightful, easy to read book, author and creator of Wicked Good Cupcakes, Tracey Noonan, confides about her roller coaster life and how she started a mega successful business with her daughter Dani. Along the way, she dishes out inspirational bits of wisdom and information. A resilient, hard working woman of integrity, she does not sugar coat entrepreneurship, but does encourage and guide the reader that may want to delve into the business world. Involvement with the Shark Tank show and a subsequent deal with Canadian businessman, Kevin O'Leary, is the highlight of the story and Noonan gives a behind the scenes look at that experience. An interesting read and very informative for an aspiring business owner." **Francesca Hawkins, Co-owner Farndale Farms and Hawkins Lumber, Pembroke, Ontario, Canada.**

"Tracey and Dani have endless tenacity and their book offers experiences that everyone can relate to and learn from with the ultimate lesson being never quit turning the pages of life! ...Keep trying no matter the obstacles and don't let the bad side of social media bring you down are such important timely messages for all. This is a really fun read loaded with inspiration for the entrepreneur and anyone that's watched Shark Tank will enjoy the inside track." **Cheryl D. Person, MAI, Owner C.D. Person Company, Sealy Texas**.

"A savvy entrepreneurial guide driven by the power of positive thinking and a never give up attitude that turned a kitchen hobby into a burgeoning commercial enterprise. The Shark Tank success is the well-deserved icing on the cupcakes!" **Leslie McDonald, author Journeys with Horses, <u>www.fcfarm.com</u>.**

"This book, like its subject matter, is a family project. What the family had in common was a willingness for hard work and a passion to learn.

Tracey attributes a lot of their success to luck, but from reading her account, it is probably more like 10% luck and 90% perspiration. Tracey and Dani both talk happily about working 14 hour days, seven days a week. To paraphrase the famous quote from Mark Twain, *if people work because they are forced to they will do as little work as possible. But if they work because they want to they will work as hard as possible.* The WGC family seems to prove his point.

Tracey, Dani and Scott spell out all the rules for making it as an entrepreneur in today's economy. Anyone who wants to try would do well by reading their instructions.

It was refreshing to see some real optimism, combined with practical advice for joy and delight. As Tracey puts it, *Don't put an expiration date on your success!"* **Steve Bartholomew, historical fiction author, <u>stevebartholomew.com</u>.**

"**A Wicked Good Idea** was very easy to follow and very easy to feel like you were there during the journey. It was amazing that they could be so upbeat throughout such trying times. Such a powerful message! Since reading **A Wicked Good Idea**, I have actually watched a couple of *Shark Tank* episodes. Wow, what a stress factor that must have been. I think they did a "wicked good" thing and I hope they have many years of happiness with their business and life. Congrats to Tracey, Scott and Dani!" **Cindy L. Hotz, Author, Michigan.**

http://www.WickedGoodCupcakes.com

For More Information Contact:

Whitehall Publishing
P.O. Box 548
Yellville, AR 72687
http://www.whitehallpublishing.com
info@whitehallpublishing.com

Tracey Noonan
http://www.WickedGoodCupcakes.com
info@WickedGoodCupcakes.com

Cover Artwork Courtesy of:
Amy Russell Farber ARFotography
http://arfotography.com/

Retail Price: $14.95

Printed in USA.

DEDICATION

This book is dedicated to all the people out there
who thought they couldn't but did.
To the people who think they can't but will anyway.
To my daughter Dani the brightest star in my life. I love you
more than you'll ever, ever know.
And to my husband Scott who believed, encouraged
and loved me through this beautiful
and wondrous process they call a start-up.

FOREWORD

Kevin O'Leary

Tracey and Dani came on *Shark Tank* with a commodity. Anyone can make a cupcake, and if you've ever seen an episode of *Shark Tank* you know that I don't like investing in anything that can be easily replicated—especially anything that can be replicated at a cheaper price.

That being said, I liked the team. One of my number one rules in business is never make decisions with your emotions, which means not investing in someone just because you like them. But Tracey and Danielle also looked like they could execute. These two radiated a tenacity that I've yet to see in some of the biggest wolves on Wall Street.

They said they need a commercial kitchen to expand their business and increase their margins. I told them I don't want equity in the family business, but said you pay me a $1 a jar until I get my money back and then pay me a royalty of 45 cents. The other sharks advised them not to do it. But they have no creativity. That's why I'm the only Shark with "Wonderful" in my name.

On the flip side, the same number of people who warned Tracey and Danielle that they'd made the wrong choice and signed a death certificate for their company thought I was making a huge mistake too. As a matter of fact, a cameraman on the *Shark Tank* set told me in between taping segments that I'd lose my shirt with this deal. He couldn't have gotten it more wrong.

The deal I made with Wicked Good Cupcakes far exceeded my expectations and our business projections. I got paid back in 74 days and will continue to collect the other royalties forever. It's a great partnership. The year before *Shark Tank* (their first year in business), they did $320,000 in gross sales. This year they'll do over four million in sales. They've gone from five employees to over 20. There are 23 million small businesses in America, and thousands upon thousands of cupcake shops and bakeries. They are the bellwether, and I can say with complete confidence that they're going to continue rising on the entrepreneurial battlefield.

Why? Because of that very tenacity I recognized in Tracey and Dani the second they stepped into the *Shark Tank*. For Wicked Good Cupcakes, that tenacity stems from a fear of being anything but successful, and it manifests in continual innovation…I always say if a business isn't innovating, it's as good as dead. I'm thrilled to say with confidence that Wicked Good Cupcakes is thriving, and Tracey and Dani are living proof that the American Dream is more alive and well than ever.

TABLE OF CONTENTS

INTRODUCTION

I'm still trying to figure out what I want to be when I "grow up." There are so many amazing things I have yet to try. Starting Wicked Good Cupcakes with Danielle and Scott was just another amazing notch in my well-worn belt of life.

I wake up every day happy to be alive, happy to be a U.S. citizen, and happy to be able to make my own decisions about who I am and where I'm going to go. The road of life is a never-ending one and I can't wait to see where it leads me today.

It all started with a cake decorating class. I wish I could give you something more dramatic than that, but that's how it happened. Our Wicked Good Idea.

And when I stop and think about the journey my daughter and I have embarked upon, it almost seems comical that we've come as far as we have.

As a 49-year-old, I wasn't looking to start a business, never mind build a nationally-recognized brand. Quite honestly, my foray into this business started out of concern for my daughter, Dani, who was struggling to find herself; dealing with depression and life as a young twenty-something.

For the last couple of years now, I've wanted to write about our story.

It's funny how you can start something a bunch of times and yet it never seems to get finished.

Why was this time the charm? Timing? More experience? A better understanding of what we're doing?

Quite possibly a combination of all those things. But mostly, I think I was finally ready. I'm at a place in my life where I understand a whole lot more than I did even just four short years ago.

If there was any piece of advice that I could offer, it would be this: Don't put an expiration date on your success! Opportunities happen for us when we are ready and not a second before. We are the sum of all of our decisions – good and bad – and that is the good news.

I used to wish that Wicked Good would have happened when I was in my 30s. But as my husband Scott so handily pointed out one day, at 30 I may not have been ready. And the opportunity that became Wicked Good may not have been there for that very reason.

On a personal note, I also feel compelled to share my back story. Growing a business is child's play in comparison to what I have lived through. My stories are sad, embarrassing and at times difficult for even me to look at and remember. But my stories are also real and genuine. You see, at the end of the day, I like to think that every decision I have made, every place I have been, every high and low point in my life, has led me to the very place I'm at today. And that's a place of happiness, promise, and love. Without all those hard times, the successes and failures we experienced would not have meant even half as much.

It's my sincerest hope that sharing our experiences in the form of business lessons *we learned* will help to encourage, inspire, and take the fear out of starting and building a business from the ground up.

The fact of the matter is that life can be rough, really rough. We are forced to make decisions, take risks, and gamble on ourselves when the options presented to us are not much better than the place we're standing in when forced to decide.

Your business or product begins right inside your head and your heart. If a mom and a daughter, both of whom didn't graduate college or have a trust fund, could accomplish this, so can you. Find your passion, roll up your sleeves, and get started. What are you waiting for?

DANI VILAGIE

Dani "Danger" Vilagie and her mother Tracey Noonan are the co-founders of Wicked Good Cupcakes. Together they have achieved the American Dream with the help of their family, the support of their community and their dedicated staff.

These days, Dani stays very busy as Director of Operations at WGC while also living a full, crazy life with her wicked hot husband Brian, their two cats and two dogs, and a bunch of four-wheelers. When she's not getting a new tattoo or dying her hair, Vilagie is out and about with mud in her tires or bingeing on Bob's Burgers.

And yes – Danger is Dani's legal middle name. She made the addition after she was married.

TRACEY NOONAN

Tracey Noonan and daughter, Dani Vilagie, are the co-founders of Wicked Good Cupcakes, Inc. Their business literally grew from their South Shore home kitchen to a nationally-recognized, multi-million-dollar brand after an appearance on ABC's *Shark Tank* and subsequent deal with Shark, Kevin O'Leary.

Now CEO of WGC, Tracey is responsible for new product development as well as collaborating on all social media content, copy writing and initiating co-branding opportunities.

Tracey has also been very involved in mentoring through Babson College's WIN lab for female MBA candidates in Boston, as well as sharing her story through various public speaking engagements. Along with daughter Dani, she is invested in animal welfare and in supporting our U.S. troops.

Recognized as a semi-finalist in the 2015 Ernst & Young Entrepreneur of the Year competition, Tracey is proud of the success of WGC and most proud of the fact that she has been able to share this journey with her family.

In her off time, Tracey enjoys playing her drums, vocal lessons, and writing screenplays. She has three Boston Terriers and lives at home with husband Scott, her parents Ed and Judy, as well as her in-laws Joyce and Gerry.

CHAPTER 1

LIFE COMES WITH
NO GUARANTEES

We are Responsible for Creating Our Own Destiny

I wanted my parents to be the wind beneath my wings, but that didn't happen. *I have come to learn that it rarely happens for anyone and for those for whom it does, I hope you truly appreciate that gift.*

I was born in 1962. My dad worked as an executive with Dr. Land of Polaroid fame. My mom stayed at home with the three kids and was your typical domestic. All very *Mad Men*-esque. I grew up middle-class and very sheltered from the outside world.

After serving in the Marine Corps, my dad attended two years of college and was off and running. My mom was a complete jock, but a terrible student. Higher education wasn't at the top of either of their lists.

I was always a bit of a loner. I loved the performing arts and shied away from the tennis courts and golf courses that my family frequented. I was quite insecure and always lived under the shadow of my athletic brothers and mom.

I can vividly remember in high school that my mom was the coach of the tennis team. It was expected that I would be a shoe-in to make the cut, but I knew my mom was a coach who wanted to win. Needless to say, I didn't even bother to try out. The good news was, it wasn't my bag to begin with.

Happily for me, I found other ways to keep myself busy.

Every day after school and all day on Saturdays I attended dance class at Boston School of Ballet. I paid for my classes with babysitting money. I took the trains in and out of the city. I did my homework late at night.

I lived and breathed dance. It was calming, it was beautiful, and it was mine. It was *my thing*.

As I passed through high school, some would argue that I missed out on a lot of trips and events that my friends went on. But that was okay. I had ballet and that was fine by me.

I can also vividly remember back to junior year in high school and all of the excitement my classmates were experiencing as they started to think about what college or university they would be attending.

Realizing that my dancing career would be limited due to the fact that I didn't start dancing until I was a young teen, I set my sights on teaching dance and to do that, I needed a degree.

My destiny was all set. Now all I needed to do was talk to my folks.

I did some research on schools and I had my ammunition ready. I waited for my dad to arrive home. After what felt like an eternity, he walked through the door and made his usual trek to the back clothes closet in our den. I followed him like a bouncing puppy. We exchanged formalities. I couldn't wait any longer. I told him I wanted to go to a performing arts school so that I would be able to teach dance…what did he think?

Apparently not much. Three sentences crushed my dream on the spot. "You're not going to college." "You're a girl; you don't need to." And, "Finish high school, get a job, and get married." And with that, he was off to reheat his dinner.

I honestly felt the lifeblood flowing out of me. That was it. And as always with my folks, he had the final word. No debate. No nothing. The answer was no.

I went to bed devastated. How could someone else determine my future? Especially someone who wasn't even going to *live* that life! My sadness turned into anger. I had to have this conversation again. And if you knew the dynamics in which I grew up, you would know this was a very ballsy move.

The following night I tried again. My father looked at me with an expression of frustration, annoyance, and exhaustion. He took a deep breath and said, "Fine. You want to go to school? You go to be a nurse or a secretary, but that's it. I won't pay for anything else."

Well, I thought I could wear him down, but he was not relenting. The more he said "no" or "this is the end of the discussion," the angrier I became. Desperate, I knew I had to take matters in my own hands.

My Plan for Success

I concocted a plan to audition at the schools I was interested in. This would require some travel. I lied to my folks and told them I was spending a weekend with friends. My mom dropped me off at the "T" (Massachusetts Bay Transportation Authority) with a suitcase and my dad's American Express card I "borrowed." I traveled to North Carolina, Virginia, and Tennessee in the course of a weekend. When I returned home, I auditioned at some local schools in Boston as a backup.

It went against the grain for me to lie and be so deceitful, but that was the depth of my desperation. I was so adamant about having the opportunity to go to school, I was willing to risk my life as I knew it, all for the chance to at least try.

A few months later, I started to receive letters from schools. I was ecstatic to learn I had been accepted to the Boston Conservatory of Music as a dance major and I had a scholarship to boot! I was in! *AND* I didn't need one red cent from my folks. Boom!

My elation was short-lived, however. Now came the task of telling my parents what I had done and what I was going to do. Yikes.

So I dropped the bomb and as you can imagine, they were furious. But it didn't matter, because I was going to school.

I moved into the dorms at the Conservatory and threw myself into my classes and studies. I had tons of like-minded friends. I felt so free living on my own and making my own decisions.

I worked on weekends teaching dance at a small neighborhood dance school in South Boston.

I performed with the Boston Opera Company, one of only two freshmen to be invited to perform. What an honor! I was thrilled, but sadly for me, my parents never saw this performance – or any performance of mine, for that matter. My short-lived life as a dancer was mine and mine alone.

Part of this was of my own making. Don't forget, I had been deceitful and this was obviously not the career path they wanted for me. In some strange way I understood. It was the choice I had to make. It sucked, but it was my way of controlling my destiny.

Life is Filled With Unexpected Challenges

Life at the Conservatory was perfect – until I made a very bad decision. I got pregnant. Yup, my high school sweetheart and I were going to be parents. And since I knew of zero pregnant prima ballerinas, it looked like my short-lived life of freedom was about to change. I finished out my freshman year at school. I went back home to my parent's house with my tail between my legs and I told them I was pregnant.

Their reaction was no real surprise. My father called me a whore and an embarrassment. My mother asked me where I was going to live, because I couldn't stay there. Hell, I had made some pretty bad decisions in my life, but this one really messed me up.

I resigned myself to the fact that unless I married my boyfriend, I was out on the street. Pissah. Wicked pissah.

A few days after breaking the news to my folks, I moved out.

I planned my wedding. I shopped for my wedding dress alone and resigned myself to the fact that I now had to change the course of my life. Gone was the dream of performing arts, a fancy wedding some day and marrying someone I was madly in love with. But there were other things I could do, right? I could power through this. Forever seemed like a long enough time to make new plans work.

Clearly there were other options I could have explored, such as having an abortion or putting the baby up for adoption, but none of those worked for me morally. I decided to take charge of this situation the way that felt right for me and for the life I had created. Yet another decision on this road of life. While every woman must make her own choice in that moment, I am grateful for the choice I made.

My husband at the time felt terrible that I had to leave school. He promised me that once he was finished with college, I could go back to school and finally have a career. It seemed doable. After all, his schooling was paid for (brilliant guy with a four-year scholarship). He'd have a job. It just might work … I put my faith and trust in the universe again and pushed forward with this new plan.

CHAPTER 2

DON'T SETTLE. EVER.

Just When I Thought I was Back on Course

Fast forward to four years later. I was now the mother of two beautiful kids living in a horrible and tiny three-room apartment in a building full of drug dealers and crazy people. While my ex worked all night, I would lie on the couch listening to strangers running up and down stairs, slamming doors, and picking up their stash. One night in a fit of rage I descended on the front porch of our building with a broom and started to whack the entourage gathered on my front stoop in an attempt to quiet down the loud chatter.

I honestly couldn't believe that this was what my life had come to. Ugh.

It had been a long, hard road, but finally the light was beginning to peek through the end of that dark and winding tunnel. My then husband had graduated and was fielding some pretty decent job offers. I was guardedly optimistic.

One evening, while he was preparing to go to his night job, I posed the question about school. When could I plan on going? Soon? This year? When? I had been patient and waited. It was my turn now, or so I thought.

Unfortunately, my husband wasn't on the same page any more. He politely told me that he would be starting his new job soon, that he was the breadwinner and I was the mother. I had two kids and that was the life I had chosen. There was no more discussion to be had.

I couldn't believe it! It was happening all over again. What the hell? Somebody else was deciding my fate for me. I stood there, completely silent, frozen, and hardly able to breathe. He kissed me goodbye and walked out the door. I don't think I moved for almost a full minute.

Completely numb, I pulled the quilted comforter off the couch, folded it into a square and placed it on the ground next to the couch. This is where my two babies slept because we didn't have a bedroom for them, never mind beds. I pulled my pillow off my bed and assumed my position on the couch like I had done every night for months. As I lay there in the dark, staring at the ceiling, I decided once and for all that I would never again allow anyone to control my destiny. My anger for allowing myself to again be caught between a rock and a hard place knew no bounds. I was done. There was no way I was staying in that sad little apartment any longer, sleeping on a couch while my kids slept on the floor. This was my rock-bottom moment.

I made yet another decision. I was going to leave and get my life back in order. I had zero idea how, but I was going to do it and no one was going to stop me ever again.

I moved out a month later.

Out of the Pan and Into the Fire

I was now definitely in for the fight of my life. I was a single mom living on $50 a week in alimony. I lost physical custody of my kids because

I had no income. I had my daughter and son two days a week and every other weekend. Ironic, isn't it, that every decision I had made for my kids ended up with me losing them? I was so angry.

Fortunately for me, I was able to channel that anger. I used that energy to push myself forward. To make opportunities where none existed. I was in for the fight of my life. Survival.

It just so happened that a neighbor of mine had purchased my grandparent's tiny ranch house in a suburb outside of Boston. And it just so happened that it was available for rent. The owner's name was Natalie.

Natalie knew me as a young child. My brothers and I played with her kids growing up. Natalie was warm, funny, and extremely loving and kind. I approached her, filled her in (honestly) about my situation, and she let me move in. Natalie never said anything to me when I was impossibly late with the rent. All she asked was that I kept the lawn mowed and the house clean, both of which I did happily.

It wasn't until many years later that I realized the power of being somebody's "Natalie." Supporting someone through a rough patch is an amazing way to help that person take the steps needed to achieve a goal or dream. At some point in our lives, we have all had a "Natalie." I challenge you to be somebody's Natalie, whether it's financially if you can or simply with kind words of support and encouragement.

When One Door Closes, a "Shutter" Opens

It was during this time I realized that I loved photography and was quite good at it. So much so, that a local photo studio in the town hired me to shoot weddings on the weekends.

I was elated that I now had some kind of a job, but knew I didn't have the right equipment to actually *do* the job. Of course, I didn't let the studio that hired me know that. F*ck. Now what was I going to do?

I accepted a job and had no equipment. This was not a good situation. I decided to bite the bullet and take a shot at an idea.

I opened up an account with American Express. I went out and bought everything that I needed in order to work. I then promptly called American Express and told them what I had done. I apologized and told them I wanted to set up a payment plan. The stunned customer rep told me I couldn't do that; I had to pay the entire bill when it came in. I politely told her that was not going to happen and she put her manager on. A payment plan was set up; my credit was hurt, but I was able to work and that was a very good thing.

After about four months of weddings, I knew that I wanted to expand my horizons. I wanted to be more than just a wedding photographer. I wanted my own business. I wanted a studio in Boston where I would shoot commercial jobs. And that's exactly what I set out to do.

The possibility of a photographic education was out of my grasp, so I did the next best thing. I went from studio to studio in Boston and tried to get myself hired as a photo assistant.

It was a brilliant idea, quite honestly. I could learn while being paid! And that's exactly what I did!

It was during this time that I met Dani's dad. He was also a photographer. We had a lot in common, or at least that's how it seemed.

I worked for him initially as a photo assistant until I was ready to start my own business. Funny, but I can still remember where we were when I announced to the universe that I was going to photograph kids for advertising.

I'm a firm believer in intention setting. I believe in visualization; "feeling the moment" and believing so hard that the "life event" actually becomes a reality.

A year and a half later I was married, had my third baby, my daughter Dani, and was on top of my game. I was one of the most sought-after commercial photographers in the city working within the niche of shooting children for advertising.

I bought a house. I took my kids to Disney World. I had horses. Life was going well.

Dani shared her thoughts about this time in the family. "Disney World is a little fuzzy, just because I was very young at the time. But I can remember going with my siblings and parents and having a blast there. We had a great time.

"That house was my favorite house still to this day, my favorite house that I've ever lived in. We had a really awesome backyard and my best friend grew up a house over from me and everything was right there for me. I definitely had a happy childhood in that house," Dani said.

And then it happened again.

Remember my lack of education? It came back to haunt me in the form of the digital age, computers, and Adobe Photoshop. That's right.

Digital photography hit the scene and literally overnight I was done. My business was an instant dinosaur.

Think about it. I didn't know how to use a computer, Photoshop, or anything related to digital photography. Film processing labs went under all around me. Friends who did nothing but color printing closed up shop. All of my clients went in-house. I can even remember where I was standing when I got the call from my biggest client telling me they were going in-house. "Sorry. We're just not going to be needing your services anymore." I was done.

I was able to limp along for about another year, but my life was once again a disaster. I split from my second husband. I sold my horses and trailer to pay bills. I sold personal belongings to buy Christmas gifts.

I even had my truck repossessed. And let me tell you, you haven't hit your lowest point until you have to meet the Repo Man in an alley in Allston, where he throws a cardboard box full of your possessions from the repossessed vehicle and calls you a "f*cking deadbeat" while you are on your hands and knees gathering up your stuff.

That was a very low day for me and unfortunately, there were more to come. Like the IRS sticking Post-it notes to the windows of my house, telling me I had to sell everything to pay them. I hid the bills in a basket so I wouldn't have to look at them, knowing full well I couldn't pay them.

Dani shared her view from a child's perspective of this time in the family. "I can definitely remember my mom had this basket that had all the bills in it and she would tell me that I could never touch that basket just in case any of the bills got lost. But I remember her saying recently that she would keep all the bills there and she wouldn't pay them, because she didn't have the money to pay them. She just kept collecting them all in this basket that she had.

"I was around seven or eight when my parents got divorced and when I was nine, I was in Catholic school at the time in Dorchester. I can remember there was this one nun there, Sister Patricia, she was not a very nice nun and she told me that my parents were going to go to hell because they got divorced. Hearing that at nine was scary, especially when you're in a Catholic school and all they do is preach about heaven and hell and the things you do.

"It was hard because [in Catholic School] we had religion tests – that's what I called them, because I had a religion class. On one of them I put that I don't believe in God, because at nine that scared me and I thought if I don't believe in God, he wouldn't take my parents away and put them in hell. And that's when my mom found out [about Sister Patricia]. So she went down to the school the next day and ripped the school apart and decided to take me out of there and put me in public schools after that. Whenever it comes to being the baby of the family or any of her children, she will tear you apart if she finds out that something's going on," Dani said.

As for the transition from Catholic school to public school, Dani said, "I was only upset because I wouldn't be seeing any of my friends anymore. I finished the school year there because it was closer to the end, so she just wanted me to ride it out and finish fourth grade there. That was fine and there really wasn't an issue. In fifth grade, she put me in Milton public schools. While it was scary, I mean, the only great thing at first was that I got to wear regular clothes all the time. I didn't have to wear my uniform, so that to me was very liberating. I was actually kind of a little relieved. Something inside felt better about leaving that [Catholic] school and I don't know if it was just because Sister Patricia ruined it for me. All the other years I was there, first through third grades were really good and then when I hit fourth grade, being with that evil nun was just awful. She wanted to do things the old-school way, like she still wanted to hit us with rulers, but she would say, 'I can't, because it's against the law now.' You know I'd be like, I don't want you to hit me."

Was this a scary time? Yes. Did I have days when it was hard to get myself going? Yes. But thankfully, I made myself have more days that were positive; more days where I could focus and work hard to get back on track not only for myself, but for my three kids.

CHAPTER 3

KEEP MOVING FORWARD AND YOU WILL FIGURE THINGS OUT

At the End of the Day I am the Only One Responsible for the Direction of My Life and for My Happiness

I think at this point God decided to take some pity on me. I met and married the love of my life, my husband Scott. We've been together for over 20 years now and I'm happy to report that I've never felt more loved, secure, and safe. I waited a long time for a relationship like this and it finally happened. I guess I always knew it would. Scott and I were married in 1998.

I met Scott in 1995. He was a horse trainer at the time and my daughters and I were among his students.

My photography business was doing great at that time and it enabled me to realize a lifelong dream of owning a horse. Well, make that two horses and a pony for the kids.

Scott was a talented equestrian with a bright future. He lived in Nice, France, and rode for the U.S. team. He rode for Moet & Chandon champagne and many other sponsors. He traveled the world and experienced so many wonderful opportunities. Scott basically had the world by the tail.

The sport of riding show jumpers requires one to be at the top of the health game. Scott, although a young man in his 20s, had been suffering with nagging back issues. He was examined several times, but no one could really find the root of the problem. Fearing the loss of his sponsors and status, Scott pushed on while in chronic pain.

One day while warming up a particularly frisky young horse in Dublin at a show, Scott suffered what would be the final blow to his international career. After a rather energetic buck and consequential hard landing back in the saddle, Scott's back broke. Literally.

And that was it. He returned home to the States to recuperate for the next year. I'm not sure to this day why he never returned to the high level of competition he had known and loved, but I guess it's no longer important. He just didn't. Scott started his training and boarding facility in the States in a small town on a beautiful 100-acre farm he leased in Wrentham, Massachusetts, where he remained for the next several years.

I met and instantly liked Scott, who was three years my junior. He was silly, smart, honest, and treated the horses with such kindness and patience. After all, who doesn't love a man who loves animals?

And animals loved him back – cats, dogs, horses, you name it. They all responded to his gentle nature and nurturing disposition.

My daughters and I would drive to Wrentham five days a week from our home in Dorchester (Boston) and lesson, ride, and have fun. It was a wonderful place and life was good.

Well, until the digital era of photography moved in, wiping out businesses and putting an end to my much-loved career.

My relationship with Dani's dad was crumbling. We suffered from money issues and tax issues, and basically realized that our goals and ambitions were not at all aligned.

As my second marriage fell apart I began to sell the horses, the horse trailer – everything that I had worked so hard to own and enjoy. My kids didn't understand what was happening. I felt like a gigantic failure again. And to make matters worse, my ex neglected to tell me that he hadn't paid our taxes for the past few years; the same taxes I signed off on, believing they were all set.

In a panic and after many Post-it notes from IRS agents on the windows of my house, I decided to sell my property. Two neighbors of ours had mentioned they were interested in our property. One of them worked for a bank. He offered me less than I had paid for the property ($208,600). I had owned the house, a lovely old Victorian with an acre of land, for three years. Surely it had to be worth more than that? I asked him for $10,000 more than I had paid. He said no. I panicked.

Scott was suffering from his own personal issues. A two-year marriage to his first wife was on the rocks. He began to hate the very industry he had built his life around. We would talk about so many things and as a result, we became close. We both had no money and life was closing in. So what did we do about it? We both got divorced from our spouses and we got married. After all, misery loves company!

Forward is the Only Option for Entrepreneurs

United as a team, we set our minds to climbing out of the financial hole we found ourselves in.

I learned *very* quickly how to make $100 a week feed five people. A fun Friday night consisted of Italian ices while snuggled in bed with our dogs and kids. Bills were prioritized. I cleaned the apartment we owned and rented for $50. We put our heads down and worked together.

And the tax issue? Scott refinanced the house, I paid the IRS and found out a few months later that our property was actually worth $500,000! That horrible neighbor knew this all along and banked on the fact that I would be forced to sell at a loss. A huge gain for him. Just another time God watched out for me and helped me through a terrible time.

It was mutually decided that I should work at the farm with Scott, mucking stalls, turning out horses, feeding and watering. It was really hard work, especially in the winter (smashing frozen water buckets, layering blankets on the horses and trudging through tons of snow), but it was a great mental break for me. I knew the work would always be there as long as we had boarders.

One early spring afternoon, Scott and I were sitting under a tree talking about future plans. Scott confided in me that he was leaving the horse world. Unknown to me, Scott had a degree in computer engineering. He knew that if the two of us were going to go anywhere in life, we needed to shift into high gear and make a move.

Part of me was actually really sad. Scott had such a gift for riding and caring for our customers' horses. But another part of me was kind of relieved. We didn't have any real financial security. We had no health insurance, no retirement, no real future. We had three kids to consider, a house to pay for and a future to build. Scott asked me to stay on at the farm alone while he readied himself to enter the business world. This would also give our customers the time to find other options for their horses and themselves. I agreed.

For the next three months I took care of the 11 remaining horses myself while Scott studied and interviewed. It was hard work. I must have fallen asleep two or three times driving back to Boston from the farm, but it was well worth it. Scott found a job with a software company. Within the first three months, he rose from developer to running the entire office, which consisted of 30 employees!

The pay wasn't great, but it was considerably more than what we had been making. I felt like the noose that had been tightening around our necks was finally loosening. We could pay our bills. We could breathe. Or so we thought.

Goddammit if it didn't happen again! Six months into his job at the software company, they decided to close the Massachusetts office. Scott was offered a transfer to the Parsippany, New Jersey, office, while everyone else was to be let go.

The move was out of the question. I had shared custody of my kids and couldn't move them out of state. Sh*t, sh*t, sh*t. Now what?

I was enrolled in massage therapy school at the time. I was working on human clients as well as equine clients. I had a nice little business, but nothing that could support five of us!

It just so happened that two fellow co-workers from Scott's firm began their own consulting business and asked Scott to join them. It was uncertain how long this new gig would last, but there were some contracts which meant work and decent pay, so Scott went to work with them.

Scott continued learning new technology trends during his consulting gig. The job lasted a year, which gave Scott enough time to bring himself up to speed within the tech industry, make some all-important contacts, and meet his new business partner. Together, he and Scott built a very successful interactive agency in Boston.

We sold our beloved and hard-fought-for home in Dorchester for over $500,000. This enabled us to breathe again and get ourselves together while I pushed forward towards finding the right career move for me.

When asked how she felt about leaving the Dorchester home, Dani said, "I don't really remember how old I was when we sold the house, but I can tell you that I was devastated when they decided to sell, because I loved that house. I just loved the location. I loved everything about the house. I was bummed that I wouldn't be able to walk next door to see my best friend anymore. I was very upset. I think I was more upset about that than anything."

"This was a very interesting time for me," said Scott. "There was a lot of stress in our lives and a lot of change happening at the same time. With all that, however, I never doubted that we would find our way to the other side. My parents raised me to be a fighter and I am grateful every day for the values they taught me. My attitude in life was quite simple; if you didn't like the way things are going, then you, and only you, must change them. That's how I viewed that time in our lives. Tracey and I wanted more for us and the kids and we were going to do whatever it took until we found the right formula.

"Ultimately, it was really a testament to the strength of our relationship and to the depth of the love we have for each other. We never let the stress of money get in the way of the joy of our family. We knew that no matter what, we'd always have each other. It didn't take money to go for a walk on the beach and simply enjoy each other's company," said Scott.

Supporting Each Other is Essential

During this time I was able to explore some different business opportunities which included an animal talent agency in Boston I started called *Animals, Animals* (fun!) and then a career as a real estate broker specializing in the niche business of equine properties.

I did well in real estate. But as my journey would have it, I, along with my customers and clients, experienced the real estate bubble burst in 2007-2008. The bottom fell out of the real estate market, creating panic and desperation. I literally felt like I was having flashbacks to all of my own financially disastrous times, as my home owners, some on the brink of foreclosure, called and e-mailed in anxiety-ridden states of mind.

I went to work getting the properties I represented sold and when the last property closed, I bid a hasty adieu to real estate. I was a great agent, but I had terrible boundaries. My client's problems became mine.

I felt like I had been through enough without taking on their issues. So once again, the search was on to find myself.

Scott's new business was on the upswing. It allowed me time to take a break, play with my horse, and figure out what it was that I wanted to do.

After two years of just hanging out, I felt the need to do something with myself. I had always enjoyed writing and storytelling. I thought that perhaps a career as a screenwriter would be a healthy and creative fit for me.

I jumped online and started to research exactly how one became a screenwriter. In the next year and a half I completed three screenplays and had a manager in Beverly Hills.

Writing. I loved it. It allowed me to be creative, to work from home and create characters whose lives were a mess, but in 90 short pages they had their happy endings. I loved my characters. I loved their stories. I totally daydreamed about seeing these stories come to life on the big screen. Which actor or actress would play my heroes? Does a screenwriter get to walk on the red carpet? I hoped so. I was all in.

But alas, it wasn't meant to be. At least not at that time. My baby, Dani, was struggling and I needed to be there for her.

Family Always Comes First

Dani's depression and lack of focus became my newest obsession.

It killed me to stand back and watch her. As a mom, I felt the need to help in whatever manner I could – even if that meant putting my life on hold for the unforeseeable future.

I have three kids. My oldest two, a 31-year-old daughter and a 30-year-old son, always seemed to have it together. My oldest daughter was a super jock, playing soccer and ice hockey as well as having attended Milton Academy, a prestigious prep school. My son was an amazing scholar and a talented drummer/musician who studied at Boston Latin.

Then there was Danielle. Dani. My youngest, now 26, who took forever to speak as a child, loved playing alone and imagining things. She was my artist, my will-o-the-wisp, my buttercup. I protected her and reveled in her different take on life. She sang, she imagined, she sculpted, and she struggled mightily in school.

By the time Dani graduated high school, it was painfully apparent that her acceptance to a community college for graphic design was not the right fit. Sadly, she had resigned herself with the hope that her course studies would grow on her. It pained me greatly, knowing the potential she possessed was somehow trapped inside of her and she just couldn't figure out how to set it free.

She was my beautiful butterfly stuck in a dark and oppressive cocoon.

Long story short, Dani left college one class shy of graduating and still searching for her calling. I was heartbroken for her. That's when my "mommy mode" kicked into high gear. I began to suggest a myriad of creative professions, even offering to help her start a refinished furniture company. I proposed driving around, finding furniture that had been discarded and rehabbing it to sell.

We had a tiny spark there. Dani found a circa-1960s television, took out the guts and turned it into a cool working fish tank. It was a great project for her and kept her mind occupied, but it was fairly obvious this wasn't her long-term passion.

During this time, Dani was dating a young man who was also struggling to "find himself." It was a toxic relationship and it added to my concerns for her. I found myself trying to lift them both up. It was stressful, exhausting, and a drain on my emotions. My efforts were clearly not working.

To make matters worse, Dani made the decision to move in with some roommates in the hopes of finding a solution to her life's quest by virtue of a change in her surroundings. In retrospect, I truly believe that I was beginning to become a nag and a constant reminder to her that she wasn't moving forward. With a very sad heart, I helped her move out and thought, *now what?*

Dani shared her take on this transition in her life. "I moved out of my house and moved in with a good friend of mine at the time. *We aren't friends anymore because I lived there.* I moved in with him because his dad had died of cancer and he had a house all to himself and he said, 'You can keep me company, move in with me.' I was only five minutes away from mom; I mean, I still lived in the same town. So I said, 'Yeah, I'll rent the room off of you. No big deal, but my boyfriend was going to come with me.' My friend said, 'Yeah, that's fine. I'll have you both move in, you can pay rent on the room and it's all good.' I lived there for 10 months and at first it was good. I was definitely experiencing some depression issues and I felt like nobody cared in that house. I felt like nobody gave a sh*t, even my boyfriend at the time. I just don't think he got it. And the environment in that house was not really a positive one. It was a typical 20-year-old's house; people came over and stayed until four in the morning. Nobody ever picked up after themselves. After living in a really clean house with mom and now with nobody cleaning up after themselves, it literally drove me f*cking crazy.

"When I first met my boyfriend I thought, *this is a really awesome guy*. I really liked him and I wanted to try and help him because he was dealing with a drug problem and I wasn't for it. I was definitely the kind of girl who thought I could take a broken dude and fix him. Now I definitely know better. When we first started dating I said, 'You can't do any more drugs because I'm totally against that and if I find out, I'll leave you because I don't want to be involved in that sh*t.' Apparently he was doing some of this behind my back and he really had anger issues, nothing bad towards me. But if he got mad, he would throw something. Of course, it would break and then he would have the bad remorse, like 'oh my God.'"

It was also around this time I had become a fan of the show *Ace of Cakes*. I loved the fondant work, the camaraderie shared between co-workers, and the potential that a business like that afforded someone. It hit me. This is it! If I could successfully introduce Dani to this profession, maybe this could be her passion and career.

I called her and invited her to take a cake decorating class with me once a week under the guise of being the mom who missed her girl. And while I did miss her, I more was excited and *very* hopeful to think that maybe this would be the spark needed to ignite her future.

Much to my sheer delight, she said yes. I'll never know if it was to appease me or maybe to get away from her current living situation, which wasn't as awesome as she had hoped. But the bottom line was that we were together once a week and I was able to support and encourage her again. And this time it took.

During this time, Dani was beginning to struggle with depression. "When I was living in my friend's house, I definitely thought I had it [depression] because there would be days when I just wouldn't want to get out of bed. I would just want to stay in my room and not go and see anybody."

Our Wednesday night classes were really fun. We learned many of the basic skills necessary to decorate a cake. I took it a step further by investigating instructional videos on YouTube that covered sculpting and working with the fondant medium, which was my interest as well as hers.

Together, we worked on projects and posted our creations on Facebook for friends and family to see.

The response was immediate. Little by little, requests came in. Can you do a dozen fireman-themed cupcakes for this? Princess-themed cakes for that? All the while, we continued to post our work on social media. People shared images and people ordered. What do you know? We had a tiny business.

We found ourselves together a lot, working on projects and enjoying each other's company. We boasted no project was too big or too small. We loved it all. We even bought a tiny chalkboard for our kitchen so we could organize orders, pickups, and deliveries. We began to buy ingredients at a wholesale club in order to save some money. Paying retail was getting expensive. My husband, Scott, posed the question: "Do you know what the cost is for each cake or cupcake you make?"

Silence ... crickets. We had no idea. I mean, we were having so much fun, we never thought we were *working*. Why did he have to ruin it for us? Dani and I were both terrible at math. I immediately had this visceral response and dodged the question every time it was asked.

For a while, that "ignorance is bliss" mentality worked – until we began to get corporate orders, that is. Yikes. Here we were, two people who were only able to bake two dozen cupcakes at a time in my home oven, when suddenly we were taking on orders of 400-plus cupcakes.

We turned a first floor spare bedroom into a holding area by installing two air-conditioning units and rolling racks. My kitchen had commercial-grade shelving all over it. We had bins of flour, sugar, and other ingredients stacked on the floor. We were growing at such a rapid rate, it was apparent we needed to ask ourselves the question: do we keep this a hobby and only take on what we could manage in our home bakery, or do we bite the bullet and really do this thing? We needed a commercial kitchen with real equipment, some experienced help and yes … we needed to know our numbers. The year was late 2010. Wicked Good Cupcakes was unofficially born.

While all of this was going on, Dani was still struggling in her personal life. "After ten months in that house, I decided to move back home and things definitely went downhill with my boyfriend. In May of that year, 2010, I had turned 21 and I went to a different liquor store and that's where I saw Brian, my future husband. I was still dating my boyfriend at the time, so I tried not to do anything with Brian, but my ex thought I was sleeping with Brian. I agreed to have no contact with Brian, but I won't lie, I did go out with him behind my ex's back. Nothing bad, we just went out for a few drinks. I wanted to escape the environment I was in with my boyfriend and I didn't know how. I thought Brian was my answer. So my ex found out that I went out with Brian and pretty much told me that I couldn't see Brian anymore or else we were done. I was trying to be good, to be the good girlfriend. So I said, 'Fine, I'll never talk to him again.'

"It was in October of that year, 2010, that my boyfriend thought I was cheating on him, so he broke up with me. To be honest, I was really relieved that he did, because our relationship was just bad. If he hadn't broken up with me, I would've broken up with him after Christmas because I was at my wit's end. I don't beg. I'm the type of girl that if we break up, we break up, there's no going back. I don't work on it. I don't care how much we're in love, I don't play that game. Once that relationship was over, I was free to talk to Brian – who ended up being my husband."

So now we are in business – kind of. We have no business plan. No idea of how to cost anything out. No real business knowledge or education of any kind.

Confident in the knowledge that it would end up with either my husband or me killing one another whenever the numbers issue reared its ugly head, I decided to investigate our local chapter of SCORE (Service Corps of Retired Executives). The thought process was that I would enlist the services offered at SCORE to show me how to develop a business plan and to help me figure out exactly what we needed to do in order to set up shop and do business the right way.

This was a really interesting time for me personally. When all of this cupcake "stuff" went down, I was working on a career as a writer. I had a fabulous manager in Beverly Hills who was helping me navigate my way around the world of writing and selling screenplays. I was happy. I loved what I was doing. And now I found myself knee-deep in cupcake batter and it really threw me for a loop. I had to face a decision that would unknowingly change my life, and my family's lives, forever.

Every night I would lie in bed and ask myself if I was going to remain a writer and let Dani figure all of this out on her own, or if I was going to invest myself in her future. Well, at least for the time being (or so I thought). We had some real momentum going. I didn't want to simply stop short of helping her reach her potential and achieve a goal, and certainly not after all we had been through. So I made the decision to put writing on the back burner and move forward with opening a cupcake shop. A simple shop in Cohasset, Massachusetts. Well, that's what I thought, anyway. And that's what we did. On October 1st, 2011, Wicked Good Cupcakes officially opened its doors. Wow. Just wow.

It was at this time that Dani decided to seek some professional help with her depression. "I finally decided to seek help when the shop opened in 2011. I wanted to talk to somebody. I went and actually started to get help for it. I started to see a psychiatrist and learned so much. I learned that if you are dealing with depression, you are not alone. I had thought I was the only one who felt this way, but quickly learned that there are millions and millions of people who suffer from it.

"Seeing the psychiatrist really does work for me. I love going to see my psychiatrist, because I can literally go there and talk about whatever the hell is bothering me and she's not going to judge me for what I have to say about it. She'll give me advice if she thinks I should do something differently, but other than that it's like the safest place I can go to vent to somebody and I feel like, as a woman, everybody needs that."

It's my sincerest hope that sharing our experiences in the form of business lessons we learned will help to encourage, inspire, and take the fear out of starting and building a business from the ground up.

I'll never sugar-coat the hard work, sacrifice and dedication that is and must be involved when achieving something great is your plan. Should you decide to strike out on this journey you will be tired, and I mean a tired like you've never known. Physically and mentally. You will struggle with little to no money, because every precious cent you make must go right back into that greedy pig you call your business. Your baby. You'll miss holidays, whether it's because you physically can't get somewhere or you don't want to because you're just too tired. You won't go on vacation for a while. (For us it was three years). You will do nothing but eat, sleep, and drink your business. And if it's your calling, your passion, your life… you'll be okay with it. Because that's what it takes.

There are no shortcuts. Your business will take the course and time it needs to take. We were fast-tracked due to an appearance on *Shark Tank*. But that posed its own set of circumstances that had to be met and dealt with. Growing a company is hard. Growing a company at warp speed is just crazy. But somehow, we survived that massive push all while remaining true to our product, brand, and each other.

And while no one who starts a business or develops a product can predict the future, you can shape and control the course your journey takes. Remember, you're in charge of your destiny and that of your company. Growing big fast shouldn't be your priority. Growing *smart* should. We've had amazing opportunities and with those opportunities came many successes and many lessons learned from things that didn't work or pan out as planned. And that's okay. If you have the opportunity to go and listen to a successful businessperson speak and they don't mention their failures along the way, then they're only giving you half their story. No one escapes mistakes and it's a fool who thinks they won't f*ck up ever.

Failure happens. To everyone. What sets you and your company apart is how you deal with these missteps. How you respond to and fix these mistakes will set you apart and help you build a strong brand.

I'm here offering to share what we have learned in the hopes that you too will see that a business can be built without an MBA or without a million-dollar investment from a venture capitalist.

Your business or product begins right inside your head and your heart. If a mom and a daughter, both of whom didn't graduate college or have a trust fund, could accomplish this, so can you. Find your passion, roll up your sleeves and get started. What are you waiting for?

That's the crazy thing about life and our journeys. They are never exactly what we plan. The trick is to be willing to bend in the breeze, to be ready to shift gears, direction, or both. And never, ever, say never! You can have the life you want, but you must not be afraid to try. This is the key. Trust me! I know.

CHAPTER 4

COMING TO TERMS WITH MY PAST

When I look back at my past experiences, it truly feels like another lifetime. Moments such as hanging colored dog biscuits on our Christmas tree because we couldn't afford to buy ornaments, only to have my Great Dane eat most of them. (True story. You could literally see the line where she couldn't reach any higher). Or baking cookies for a women's homeless shelter in Boston, only to have them think we were there for dinner. All of these moments defined me.

Remember, all of the experiences, especially the negative ones, contributed to making me the me I am now.

The same holds true for my exes. I felt anger and disappointment, frustration, even hate. But I know they felt the same as well. I can't blame anyone else for my actions because they were just that. Mine.

As an adult, I'm actually able to see that all of the defining moments were actually *on me* in some way or another. Hanging on to hate and blame stops us from moving forward. It prevents us from creating the change that is necessary to simply move on. If I continually looked in my life's rearview mirror, I could never have progressed towards the future. Clichéd I know, but honestly, very true. I've given up being angry and upset when things don't immediately work out the way I think they should. I've repeatedly learned over and over again that the best route for me just hasn't presented itself yet. I am living proof that things happen for a reason. And the best is yet to come. It really is!

Then and Now

Fast forward to my life now. I'm proud to say I've experienced a myriad of careers that I've enjoyed and achieved some measure of success in. I've owned and trained animals for my Animal Talent Agency in Boston called **Animals, Animals**. I've worked on movies, television shows and still photo shoots. I've been a human and equine massage therapist and I have written and completed three screenplays.

I've let go of my anger and disappointment with my parents. As an adult, I see and understand the place they were coming from. They lived in a very different time and only acted the way that they knew how. Nothing was ever done with the intention of hurting me. I know they had hopes and dreams for me and in their eyes I let them down as much as I felt they let me down. Were my plans different from theirs? Yup. At the time there was no changing their minds, or mine, for that matter. Those were the cards I was dealt.

And even though I can look back and understand why my dad was the way he was, I made a promise to myself that my children would grow up with the belief that they could do and be anything they set their minds to. And furthermore, they would have my undying support.

Dani shared one of her favorite memories of her mom's commitment to provide undying support to her kids, especially when she didn't agree with their choices. "I was a goth kid and she hated that. No parent likes it, actually. Nobody wanted to have a goth kid, but she was very, very supportive of me having that lifestyle for a little bit and I would always tell her 'It's just a phase; I'll grow out of it when I get older, but right now in high school I don't want to be the preppy cheerleader, I want to be the goth kid.' It never changed my attitude. I was always very honest and bubbly, I just preferred the black clothing. I just liked the style. I liked the music.

"I can remember her going shopping for me. One day, she went to a shop that specialized in goth clothing and she was with my Nana. My mom was picking up some outfits for me because she always knew what I liked. She was always really good with that and my Nana would ask, 'Why are you buying her these clothes?' My mom would just look at her and say, 'It's okay if this is what she wants to do right now, fine, she is not hurting anybody or hurting herself and when she grows out of it, she grows out of it.' I always thank my mom so much for understanding that this was just who I wanted to be for the time being. I have since grown out of that phase in my life, but I will always be grateful to my mom for allowing me to be myself."

Our children have the promise of their futures. Who are we to stand in their way? This can be especially difficult if the path you are envisioning is headed the way of disaster. Ask yourself, "Is this going to end up with their demise?" If not, as hard as it may be, let them make the decision and learn from the mistakes that will ensue. And who knows? Maybe the decision will work out in their favor. Your role as a parent is to support, guide, forgive, and love – not to dominate and control.

Our children have the freedom this country affords everyone, men and women, to be able to choose a career where they could feel happy, fulfilled, and important.

When asked how Dani would raise her children differently than her mother did, she said, "I would follow a lot of what my mom did because what she did was for us and I want to be the kind of mother that she was."

You are Never Too Old for a New Beginning

That's life. How to deal with life as it happens, ready or not.

I believe I've mentioned somewhere along the line that I am not a spring chicken. When we started Wicked Good I was already 49 years old. I was also working furiously to establish myself as a writer of screenplays. This was not my first career change.

I've been through two divorces, several businesses and a myriad of health issues. And while I managed to struggle my way through all of these hardships, nothing could prepare me for the life-altering event that has become my reality now.

My mom, Judy, and dad, Ed, moved back to Massachusetts in 2014. Both parents were suffering from memory/brain-related issues. My dad was diagnosed with Alzheimer's disease and my mom with dementia.

As you can imagine, it was a shock to us and we needed to immediately gain control of their lives that had been freewheeling out of control in Florida. My brothers and I have delegated duties, but it has been a logistical challenge for all of us, to say the least.

I have found myself driving to our Cohasset office only to have to divert myself from my route in order to stop by their apartment to aid them with an issue that's pressing, at least for them.

As their only daughter, I feel especially compelled to assume the role of caretaker. I'm sure every woman reading this can relate to these emotions, whether they have a young family or they're older like me and have aging parents looming on the horizon.

I find that a good portion of my day is being sliced into work, home, parents, kids, grandkids, husband, dogs, and then me.

I wish I knew the magic formula needed to make all of this work seamlessly, peacefully, and effortlessly. I'm afraid that this magic bullet does not exist. So what's a girl to do? Sigh. There's no perfect answer for that either. The approach I took was this:

I decided to take charge of my destiny. My parents were here and this issue wasn't going away. I made a list of all the challenges I was facing. The common denominator was time wasted. If I could have them with me all the time, then I could answer questions, problem solve, attend doctor's appointments, and make sure they were eating. So on and so on. They needed to live with us.

Enter my very understanding husband. Armed with a list of pros and cons, we discussed the good and difficult points of a living situation like this. Trust me. We didn't sugar-coat anything. No question was off limits as we delved into any and all scenarios. Soul searching became my second hobby.

After weeks of number running, family meetings, and honest talk between Scott and myself, we decided that we would invite my parents to live with us. And while we were at it, we invited his parents as well. Why not? They were living alone up in Vermont and getting to them was a real problem. On January 28th of 2015, we bought a home in the lovely seaside town of Marshfield, Massachusetts, on the South Shore.

My dad's Alzheimer's has rapidly advanced. Some days I don't even want to see him because it makes me so sad to see the blank expression behind his blue eyes. Don't get me wrong; we've had a very tenuous relationship throughout our lifetime. I constantly struggle with the emotions of anger, sorrow, frustration, and pity. All I ever wanted to do was impress my dad. To show him that I could be something, even though I had totally f*cked up in his eyes.

Enter life's irony. Now that I've succeeded, he simply doesn't understand. It figures. It has to be enough that *I know*. And that my success pays his bills and keeps him warm and safe.

You see, dear friends, life happens. Even with the best-laid plans. And being able to react in a compassionate, thoughtful, and practical manner can put you in a better place in which to deal with personal crises while running your business. None of us escapes tragedy, strife, and stress. But if we have contingency plans in place, honestly assess the plans we think will work, and bring in family and friends for support, then you can live a decent life, care for those you love, all while maintaining a healthy, thriving business.

Remember, if you're not mentally in balance, there's no way your company can be. Life has a way of throwing sh*t at us when we least expect it. Do me a favor and take care of yourself. Please.

CHAPTER 5

WICKED GOOD CUPCAKES IS BORN

From Humble Beginnings

My daughter and I are often asked the same question: "How did you start your business?"

I always give people the same reply. I tell them it just kind of happened on its own organically. There was no business plan, no forecasts, no anything. At least not to start. We were just a mother and daughter sharing time once a week at a cake decorating class.

I also always get the same almost disappointed look from people when I answer them. I don't know if they expected something more exciting or if there was another response they were waiting for.

The intention of this section of the book is to chronicle how we grew our business and the very important lessons we learned – literally on the fly sometimes!

I am not a hard-core business author or guru. I don't have an MBA or even a college degree. But I can share real life experiences that Dani and I worked through as we grew our brand.

In the beginning, our business grew slowly and on its own. We had no idea the path we had started down. I think Mark Twain described me and Dani best when he said, "In order to succeed you need two things;

ignorance and confidence." That described the two of us perfectly; ignorant about the fact that we were soon going to be working *really* hard, but confident we had a great product.

It actually wasn't until people began to request our product, pay for that product, and then request more product again that it sunk in. "How cool is this?" we thought. People are willing to pay us to do the very thing we enjoy doing together!

Growth Often Comes in Baby Steps

When Dani and I started Wicked Good Cupcakes, we had a cute shop in the South Shore seaside town of Cohasset, Massachusetts.

The day we opened our doors for the first time in October of 2011, we had a line out the door and sold over 1,000 cupcakes.

We were really fortunate to have chosen such a tight-knit community as Cohasset. Word of our shop spread like wildfire before we even opened our doors! With the help of the local press we had an amazing welcome from the town.

Needless to say it was a huge success. I was overwhelmed and terrified. I think I quit around 2:00 p.m. that first day.

We had all kinds of help. Family and friends manned the register and counter. My in-laws even washed dishes.

We could barely keep up. All I could think about was how tired I was and that we were going to have to do this all over again the next day.

Scott was thrilled with the response we received. People literally came back two and three times the first day! He immediately saw the potential if we could somehow hit the scene nationally.

With Growth Comes Growing Pains

Yup. Here is an inevitable fact: you and your business are about to become best friends.

Remember way back when I told you that the reason we started cake decorating was so that Dani and I could spend more time together? Well, be careful what you wish for.

As our business started to find its groove, Dani and I spent lots of time together. Like 15 to 18 hours a day together, six days a week. We opened and closed. We baked, decorated, counted money, scrubbed floors, emptied the trash, washed dishes, scheduled our few employees … you get the gist. We *were* our business. And for as much as we were confident we had the best product, the growth of our company was going to take as long as it was going to take. No amount of being dedicated, brilliant, or being there all the time would speed things up. Our business just needed to follow the path it was going to take. But that was okay. We were working and learning. Every day had something new to teach us.

Looking at this family relationship from Dani's point of view, she had this to say: "I liked it, because I was 22 when we started the shop and I was one of the owners as well as one of the youngest people in the building. As a 22-year-old I appreciated the idea that if I made a mistake, I wasn't going to get fired! However, as one of the owners, I also wasn't cut any slack. No one treated me special because I was the daughter. I had to work a lot. I really didn't get any special treatment from anyone. I feel like my employees were treated better than I was, because I was considered one of the owners and I had to put in 110 per cent whether I wanted to or not. It was very hard to work that way, I guess.

"One of the challenges was definitely working with some of the people I had at the time. I was inexperienced in the baking world and I was younger than the majority of everybody. So it was really hard to rope them in and say, 'take me seriously.'"

Everything they say about business taking five years to show a profit and to be secure is true. (Unless you have the good fortune of meeting a wonderful Shark, but that's a story for another section.)

If you're not 100 per cent completely passionate about what you're planning on doing for a business, don't do it.

If you don't have the patience to work with little reward and the balls to take a whole lot of risk to start, don't do it.

If you're in it just to make money and be a millionaire overnight, don't do it.

If you love your social life and will have a hard time giving up free time, vacations, and days off, don't do it.

Your business is going to become your focus, your worry, your baby, your obsession … your life.

To this day I can remember driving home late while struggling to stay awake. I remember taking on custom jobs that required us to stay long after closing to do intricate fondant work because that was the only time we could find in what was a very long day. I remember telling family we couldn't make a holiday dinner because we had to work. Again.

There's nothing wrong with making the difficult decision that maybe owning and operating your own business just isn't for you. I really believe that ignorance is bliss, because I'm not sure I would have decided to move forward with our business had I known just how much work it was truly going to be.

What *would* be wrong would be jumping into something only to find out six months down the road that you're miserable, in debt, and have no way out. Putting yourself and your family in that kind of jeopardy isn't fair to anyone. Not everyone is cut out to be their own boss and that's okay. Remember, if it was easy, everyone would do it!

And while we dragged our very tired butts to work each day, orders kept rolling in. So much so that we reached a point where a critical decision needed to be made. Do we keep baking out of the kitchen (impractical, really) or do we roll the dice and try to grow this thing? (*So* f*cking scary.)

Show of hands. How many of you reading this right now have thought about starting your own business?

And out of those with hands raised, how many of you have gotten to the point of almost quitting your current job?

How many of you are scared as hell at the very thought, but are super excited at the same time? Thought so. We felt the same way.

Looking back now, the three most important questions anyone should ask themselves before diving into a business had been answered for us. So here they are ... consider your own answers before you jump ship at your current place of employment and invest every penny you've ever saved into your new baby.

1) Are you truly passionate about your product/service?

This is a tough one. You need to have a clear-cut understanding of the level of passion that one must possess before diving in.

My husband Scott defines this passion perfectly. He describes it as *Will vs. Want.*

Allow me to quote him. "Being an entrepreneur is a lot like training for and running a marathon. In all the books we read and seminars we attend, we constantly hear the same thing. To be successful, you must be ***willing*** to sacrifice, ***willing*** to work long hours for little pay, ***willing*** to take time away from your family. To me, being ***willing*** to do something and ***wanting*** to do something are very different. If, at the root, you don't have the passion or the ***want***, all the ***will*** in the world is not enough to carry you through."

When Dani and I first started our company, we didn't take any pay for the first year. ONE YEAR. Every cent went back into our business, whether it was to pay an employee, buy a much-needed piece of equipment, or pay a bill. Dani moved back home because she could no longer afford to live on her own. My husband, Scott, and I cut back on dinners out.

(Half the time I was too tired to even make the effort to clean myself up even if we could go out!) We missed birthdays, anniversaries, holidays with family. Our entire existence was our work. We lived, breathed, and slept Wicked Good Cupcakes.

There were nights when I had to stay after closing to work on a custom cake project, creating fondant characters that only I could do. I still remember driving home past 10:00 or 11:00 p.m. and even falling asleep at the wheel once or twice. But come the morning, I was ready to go back to it again because I loved what we did and I wanted to make everyone who walked through our door happy. Which leads me to question number two.

2) Can you be the best in the world at what you do?

Yup. You have beautiful, hand-knit nose warmers. No one else knits like you. Friends and family tell you this all the time. But have any of these so-called admirers ever paid for your nose warmers? Have they ordered some for friends?

What's different about your product? And I mean *really* different; not just you saying you're the best. Your gorgeous nose warmers, much like our delicious cupcake jars, are a commodity. Commodities can be replicated by many people, as they're not protected by a patent. And since you have a product that others can copy, you must show your prospective buyers why they should purchase *your* nose warmers over someone else's. And the way you do that is by having a differentiator.

A differentiator is defined by businessdictionary.com as such: Unique features and/or benefits of a product, or aspects of a brand, that set it apart from competing products or brands.

In a nutshell … you need to have a new twist or angle. I can't tell you how many times people would say "Another cupcake company?" Yes. Another cupcake company. We are a commodity. But so are hundreds of other products. I have a feeling that the people who turn their noses up at commodities are the ones who don't understand that commodities are the backbone of the American economy. And to take this thought one step further: can you even imagine living in a place that only offered you one brand of something?

If we lived in a place (the former Soviet Union) that only had one car company, one appliance company, even one brand of cookie, what motivation would there be for the company that holds the monopoly on any of these businesses to continue to improve their product? Mediocrity would run rampant.

Competition is key for providing the populace with the opportunity to buy or use the very best product or service. Competition fuels business and that keeps everyone on the straight and narrow.

Let's take, for example, ice cream. When Ben & Jerry's hit the scene, there were hundreds of other ice cream companies/shops. But they had a differentiator. And it wasn't just that they had a great product.

While we were in the *Shark Tank* being grilled by those savvy investors, our own Mr. Wonderful posed that very question. Why should anyone buy a cupcake from us when there were so many other cupcake shops out there? Great question. You better believe I was ready for that.

I started by answering with the history of Ben & Jerry's Ice Cream. Here were two hippies who took a $10 mail order correspondence course about how to make ice cream. They used only the best ingredients, worked with local farmers, and drove around in a beat-up van selling their ice cream. They were socially responsible and stood their ground even in the face of a corporate takedown.

In a nutshell, Ben & Jerry's had moved their ice cream out of their scoop stores and into the highly-competitive world of supermarket share. Around the same time, Pillsbury bought Häagen-Dazs for the tidy sum of 70 million dollars from immigrant Rueben Mattus and his wife Rose. (Go Mattus!)

As you may imagine, Pillsbury had a lot at stake and didn't want the two hippies from Vermont competing with their new acquisition.

When Ben & Jerry's expanded to Boston, Pillsbury threatened distributors that if they didn't make Pillsbury the *only* premium ice cream available in Boston, they would pull their product off the shelves, causing the supermarkets to lose a ton of ice cream sales. Literally. Pillsbury gave the distributors a deadline. A line was drawn in the sand and Ben & Jerry's loved it. They laced up their gloves and promised not to go down without a fight.

The long and short of the story was based on this slogan: "What's the doughboy afraid of?" They challenged Pillsbury, a faceless corporation, rather than getting into a fight with Häagen-Dazs, another ice cream company. Yup. Two hippies took on the Fortune 500 company.

Ben & Jerry's took out ads and plastered this slogan on the sides of buses, on tee shirts, even in *Rolling Stone* magazine. They printed a 1-800 number on the sides of their cartons, where people could call for more information and learn all about the whole debate.

Ben & Jerry's successfully painted themselves as the underdog, garnering headlines in the *Boston Globe* and the *Wall Street Journal* referring to this incident as "David vs. Goliath."

As the deadline approached and passed, Pillsbury reluctantly entered into months and months of negotiations, ultimately allowing stores to carry both products, all while convincing Ben & Jerry's to take the 1-800 number off their ice cream cartons.

All of this garnered more PR for Ben & Jerry's than months of advertising ever could.

When you can, go to this link and read the infamous article: http://thinkofthat.net/2009/10/20/whats-the-doughboy-afraid-of/. Fascinating stuff – and what a differentiator!

Now relate the idea of a differentiator to you and your business.

I know. I know. I can hear you now. You knit using the finest yarns, spun by vestal virgins. Awesome! Using quality ingredients or products is definitely a start, but not the way to answer someone like a Mr. Wonderful. He'll call you out and tell you he can hire someone to buy fabulous ingredients and make great quality cupcakes (or nose warmers), too.

This is the point where we hooked him. Much like Ben & Jerry's, we not only had an outstanding product, but we had a great back-story. Here's a mother and daughter with no business backgrounds, and no real money to speak of, whose sole purpose was to share some time together. And yet look at what they did! And it didn't stop there. Not only did we have a great product and a great story, but we had a differentiator. More on that in the next section!

And finally question number three.

3) Will people be willing to pay for what you make/do?

Whether you have a product or a service, in order to make your dream a reality you need to know that people will be willing to pay for it. And to take it a step further, will they be so happy that they come back again? You definitely need to be on top of your game if you expect people to buy your product or use your service again. If you're a one-hit wonder, you'll die a very quick death.

Those nose warmers need to be a product that people love, use, and finally can't imagine living or being without. If you don't provide your customers with an easy ordering experience, good customer service, and the quality they expect, they'll never come back again. And don't be foolish enough to think that just because someone doesn't reach out with a complaint that there are none. Most people won't bother letting you know they were disappointed. They simply won't come back. Oh! And the few who do complain will definitely let you know how they feel. Trust me.

Yes. Selling, repeat business, and then eventually supporting yourself is an important step in any young business.

Finding our Road to Success

So Scott went to work doing what he did best and built us a website. He used his expertise in SEO (search engine optimization) and we had a small but consistently growing audience who asked us when we were going to ship our product nationwide.

Good question. How would we accomplish that? What would we need? Packaging? Ice? UPS? FedEx? Systems? So much to think about.

We started ordering from our "online competitors." We examined pricing, packaging, and the all-important quality of the product when it arrived. We weren't impressed. Once the cupcakes thawed, the sprinkles on top melted. The cupcakes looked like sad clowns. Packaging squashed. Product was stale.

I wasn't on board with the whole shipping thing. I knew that people were spending a lot of money to ship a dozen cupcakes as gifts and I knew they would be disappointed with what was arriving if we shipped our cupcakes the same way everyone else was.

This was definitely going to be a tough nut to crack.

We're always asked who came up with the idea to use the mason jar, which became the differentiator for us. I wish I could say it was me or Dani, but the truth of the matter is that it was Scott's idea – an idea he came up with while watching television in the middle of the night and coming across a show about canning. That was the moment.

We had a problem that we needed to solve. We had a commodity that needed a differentiator. The mason jar was it.

By using a mason jar, we were able to extend the shelf life of the cupcake while keeping it protected during shipping.

As I mentioned, Scott saw this canning show in the middle of the night. He was so excited that he woke me out of a dead sleep to fill me in. I was not so excited. I actually told him he was f*cking crazy and to never wake me at 1:00 a.m. again unless the house was burning down.

Thankfully for us, he was persistent about the idea. In an attempt to shut him up, I agreed to beta test the idea and send jars to family and friends across the country to see what they thought of it, and how the jars would arrive.

I wrapped the jars in bubble wrap (we didn't have our packaging at that time) and sent them via the postal service. Much to my surprise, people really loved them!

Maybe Scott was actually on to something. We had our differentiator. This concept just might work!

That was the first step. Now we had to decide what flavors, how many layers of cake and frosting and how to make these pretty. They were going to be gifts, after all.

We decided to try and get the jars on our website for that first Christmas (remember, we opened October 1st).

The Anything-but-Glamorous Minutiae

I was being my usual Type A self and was insistent upon the fact that I was the only one who could make these jars perfectly and beautifully. I hot-glued ribbon on the jars. It took me all day to do almost 30 jars; not exactly the model of efficiency. No matter where you start, if you keep moving forward and are willing to change direction when something doesn't work, you will get there.

Scott was hoping that we could sell enough of these bad boys to pay our monthly rent, which at the time was $3,000. A lofty goal indeed.

After finally admitting defeat and that my way of doing things was not efficient enough to allow us to reach our $3000-a-month goal, we made some changes to simplify the process.

Instead of hot-gluing bows, we bought ready-tied, metallic elastic bows that we just snapped on. There. That saved a lot of time! We were still wrapping jars in bubble wrap and packing them in boxes with a hay-like product called Wonder Wood. And while the jars looked cute in their little "nests," the Wonder Wood got everywhere and created a huge mess in the packing area.

We also were spending way too much money on our mason jars. In the beginning, we were purchasing them at retail through a local supermarket. This would be the death of us if we continued this way.

So now I had to settle on packaging, find wholesale mason jars, find a way to label the jars, and have them tested at a lab as required by the state. Jars could not be shipped across state lines without this information that had to be provided to the state in order for us to obtain our wholesale license.

Wholesale license? Weights of the product? Ingredients and *sub*-ingredients? Who knew? Not us. It was baptism by fire, baby, and we had to learn fast.

We soft-launched our cupcake jars online at the beginning of December, 2011. The orders trickled in slowly. I began to spend my slower times at the shop researching packaging online, which was no easy task because I had no idea what I was actually looking for. I just knew the bubble wrap and Wonder Wood wasn't sustainable if this were to take off.

I finally found a Styrofoam company in New Hampshire who was intrigued and invited me to their office for a tour and meeting.

I found out that the Ball jars we were using were brokered by a company other than Ball. I set up an account. In the meantime, we continued to buy jars at our local market.

We developed a system for filling the jars. We offered five flavors. We struggled to do 75 jars a day. (To put this into some perspective, we now do 10,000 jars a day in our busy season and that's because that's all we can do in our current production situation!)

We kept innovating. We would constantly tweak the process. Our labels changed. Our flavor menu grew.

Scott built systems for our website in order to make the process easier for our customers and more organized for us.

When I look back at everything now, it exhausts me. Thank God we didn't know what we didn't know. I'm not sure I could have stuck it out. Ignorance truly was bliss.

The TSA Helps WGC

Our initial hope for the cupcake jars was that we'd sell enough of them to cover our $3,000-a-month rent.

They began to sell, little by little. We gave our customers the opportunity to include a gift card. Dani or I would handwrite the message for the customers and include them in the package.

We had one particular order – I actually remember writing the card – from a student to his Communications professor at Salem State

University. He sent her a two-pack and thanked her for helping him with his resumé.

Little did we know that this particular order would be the ignition for our epic lift-off!

About two weeks later, as I settled in at work to answer e-mails, I received one from the student who had sent the cupcake jars. Attached to the e-mail was a post from the website Boing Boing. The post had a photo of a TSA agent in Las Vegas' McCarran Airport holding one of our Red Velvet cupcake jars.

The message read something to the effect of, "Hey there. I ordered some jars for a professor of mine and she had it confiscated at McCarran Airport. The TSA deemed you a national security threat."

Well, after laughing hysterically I called Scott, who was at his former job, and asked if he thought it was a newsworthy story. He said exactly what I thought he would. "Hell yeah." I called our local ABC news affiliate.

What do you know? It turned out that the story actually had legs and quickly became an international story. News stations, late-night talk show hosts … everyone was talking about our cupcake jars with the "gelatinous substance" that the TSA deemed as a national security threat. Yeah, that was the frosting.

Needless to say, it gave us a good little boost going into Christmas. People even reordered and that was very cool. It was near the end of December and the Department of Homeland Security had been on our website 200-plus times. It was funny, but also a little unsettling. I mean, after all, it's not every day you and your daughter are considered to be a national security threat!

In January, the TSA in their infinite wisdom retracted their position and made the bold statement that our cupcake jars *were not your run-of-the-mill cupcakes.* Another home run for Wicked Good! This newest wave carried us through Valentine's Day. We scrambled to fill orders.

Because we had no real systems in place, we were lucky if we could bake, assemble, pack, and ship 75 cupcake jars a day. But I knew we could figure it out. There was no way I wasn't going to take any and all orders that were coming in! My mantra has always been, "Say yes now and figure the rest out later."

Reorders kept happening. Daily orders crept upwards ever so slowly. What was happening?

Had we found our differentiator? It was definitely looking that way.

Surprise Lessons Learned

Owning and operating Wicked Good Cupcakes has taught me about patience. It's taught me how to handle and look at disappointment in many different ways. I've learned about my family members having worked in very "close quarters" and in an intimate way that one can only know when sharing dreams, work, sweat, and tears.

I've learned about forgiveness. I've forgiven others, but more importantly, I've learned to forgive myself.

I'm not a perfect person, wife or mom. And that's okay. Neither are any of the others around me each and every day. Being able to forgive is the first step towards being free and truly being happy. No longer am I bogged down with feelings of anger or hate. I needed to focus my energies on the positive. And in doing so, success has come to me.

What Does Courage Look Like?

My husband Scott and I have recently opened our home to both sets of parents in 2015.

As I previously mentioned, my dad suffers from Alzheimer's disease. My mom from dementia and a heart condition.

Scott's dad is battling bone cancer. His mom suffers from degenerative spine disease.

Why have them move in? The answer is simple. Because at this point we can, but even more importantly, because it's the right thing to do. Family is all we have at the end of the day.

What good is all the money and success if you cannot use it to help someone?

Is it hard? Oh yes. It's definitely life-changing. There are times when I feel like I just want to be alone with Scott. But when I look at my dad in his frail and forgetful state, I think to myself, at one point he was somebody's little boy. I don't know why I think that. It could be from the role reversal I've experienced. At any rate, that thought helps me to be more empathetic and feel less frustrated.

Life is a crazy thing. I've found you can plan and plan and try to force things to work, but ultimately, you are going to follow the path you are destined to follow. You must control that destiny.

You must also control your fear. So many people try something, fail, and get up and try again the next day. These are the people who are controlling their destinies. And while their lives may feel out of control at certain points, that's hardly the case. By taking a risk, making opportunities, and by being brave, you are forging your path to success.

I've had good times and I've had really sh*tty times. This will continue to be the case until the day they put me in the ground. I will get up every day and make decisions that will either work or not. The fact that I know I am human and will fail at things doesn't deter me from living and moving forward.

Quite the opposite. I'm grateful for each and every day. I'm grateful for all of the experiences I have had and learned from. I am the sum of all my parts – the good, the bad, and the ugly. I embody a wonderful, albeit challenging, life and so do you.

If there is an opportunity that could prove to be a good thing for me, my family, or my business, you better believe I'm going to go for it. I would rather live with the fact that I took a chance and tried even if it didn't pan out, rather than having to live with the nagging regret of "what if?"

Regret is a terrible thing to live with. Don't let that be your legacy.

www.WickedGoodCupcakes.com

CHAPTER 6

APPLYING TO SHARK TANK

What do You Have to Lose?

Ask yourself this question when an opportunity arises and you're on the fence. "What do I have to lose?" Even if this opportunity doesn't work out, it has put you one step closer to another that will!

I truly believe with all my heart and soul that every decision I have made, every path I've followed, and every opportunity that has presented itself to me has led me to this very spot where I stand today. And where I stand today is a very happy place.

This philosophy is one I apply to my personal life as well as my business life. There are so many things I have yet to try, so many places I have yet to visit.

I feel like every day I wake up is one more day on this beautiful earth to make a new path, experience a new adventure and a new day to be grateful for all the other days I have suffered through in my past. Grateful? Why? Because those events have made me the best me I can be and without every one of those, I wouldn't enjoy or be as grateful for all that I have now in my life.

What have you got to lose? The worst that can happen is that you fall flat on your face and I've already had the pleasure of doing that more than one time (first marriage, photo biz), and I now know what doesn't kill you, makes you stronger.

Judge a book by its character. Both Kevin O'Leary and Marcus Lemonis have great character, no matter what their critics may say.

"You're so lucky," people often say to me. I guess in some ways I am. I'm a woman who owns a business in a country where women can be business owners without fear of persecution. I live in a country where anything is possible if you are willing to work hard, take risks, and own the outcome, good or bad.

I have a wonderful family. I'm in great health. I live in a nice house near the ocean. I take care of my parents. I have dogs that bring me incredible amounts of joy. They're my little angels in fur pants. And I play the drums when I can.

Yup. Pretty lucky. But I'd be willing to bet that's not what they're referring to. The luck they speak of is in regards to Dani and my opportunity to appear on ABC's hit show, *Shark Tank*.

I have to honestly admit that phrase used to make me mad. I'd respond back with, "Yes. I'm lucky that I work hard." The way I look at it is we didn't do anything anyone else couldn't do. There's no secret sauce here. Anybody can go to the following link http://abc.go.com/shows/shark-tank/apply and apply.

And eight months into our business that's exactly what I did; me and 45,000 other hopeful entrepreneurs. I think the luck we had wasn't in getting on the show as much as opportunities along the way that led up to me applying for the show.

CHAPTER 7

SWIMMING WITH THE SHARKS

I Can do Anything I Set my Mind to
…and So Can You

In April of 2012, I applied to *Shark Tank*. Honestly, it happened with me saying to myself, "Oh, yeah. I should apply to *Shark Tank* today before I forget again."

We have always been big fans of the show. I had been dying for the opportunity to appear on there. Imagine what we could do with the backing and brains of a billionaire investor. The sky would be the limit. I simply had to try. So on one fateful day I took the plunge and answered the very short questionnaire.

About five days after I applied, I had a message on my voicemail from Mindy from *Shark Tank* casting. I honestly couldn't believe it. I called Scott immediately. He was equally as surprised.

I got in touch with Mindy (love her!) and apparently our phone interview went well. She mailed us out the formal application packet. Tons and tons of pages of stuff. We also had to create an unedited video with us talking about our business. We were so excited, we missed the "unedited" part in the instructions and created a fun video that showcased Dani's and my personalities. Oops. At the end we talked about what being on the show would mean to us. With fingers crossed, we sent everything off and waited to hear back.

Yay! A few weeks later we heard back! They loved our video and wanted to move forward.

At the end of May, 2012, we were assigned our production team led by producer Heather (love her too!). Heather and her assistant Ben spoke with us weekly and prepped us for what we could expect should we be lucky enough to fly out to Los Angeles to tape.

Yup. You read correctly. The big *if.* You see, with *Shark Tank* comes *no* guarantees. There is no guarantee they'll fly you out and if they do, there's no guarantee that you'll get in front of the Sharks. No guarantee if you do tape that you'll get a deal or end up on air. Nothing.

We flew to Los Angeles the day of my 50th birthday. My family, for the life of them, couldn't figure out why my husband wasn't throwing me a 50th birthday party. We lived for the next nine months, literally day-to-day waiting and hoping that we would hear that we were chosen and that we had an air date. (Again, no guarantee you'll air until the show is signing on). This was incredibly nerve-wracking. Top all of that off with the fact that we signed a five-million-dollar NDA (non-disclosure agreement). Yup. So you can't tell *anyone.*

The only people who knew we had applied to the show were Scott, Dani, myself, and a few of our employees. That was it. Imagine keeping something like that a secret!

I'm bound legally not to disclose a lot of what happens during the *Shark Tank* process, but what I can tell you is this: Sony/Disney/ABC treated us like gold.

We stayed in a very nice hotel with the other entrepreneurs scheduled to tape. No one is allowed to talk about what it was they did for work. We all traveled in vans together, kind of like a cult. We arrived on a Saturday. Sunday night we had to do our pitch for the network execs. Imagine standing in a room in front of about 30 people all typing on laptops while you launch into your pitch. How you did that night played a part in determining if you went forward. But no pressure …

I can remember when we finished that practice pitch, we had to go back to our room and wait for "the call" to see if we were slotted to pitch.

We had the good fortune (okay, *luck*) of landing the spot right before the Shark's lunch break. Perfect for us, because we had food!

We had Monday as an off day, so Dani and I went to Venice Beach and walked to the Santa Monica Pier. Neither of us had been to the West Coast before. We promised each other that no matter what happened, we would take away only the good and appreciate everything we were given to experience. This was to be a learning experience.

As a mom, this was nirvana. We had the time of our lives and created a memory that only Dani and I share. It was exciting, scary, and mentally exhausting. We were in front of the Sharks for 45-60 minutes, although it felt much faster than that. We even called Scott when Kevin made the royalty offer, because I just wasn't sure. That call was edited out and from what I understand it was the most intense two hours for him, as he was on standby right before we went in and throughout our pitch. I can't even imagine waiting and not knowing what was going on.

Scott may have had the hardest day of all of us! "As far as Tracey and Dani's filming of *Shark Tank*, I would say I was more anxious than nervous," said Scott. "I took the day off from work and hung out at the bakery with the rest of the employees. They thought I was there to fill in for Tracey and Dani, who were at a trade show (or so they were told ☺).

"Back in those days, *Shark Tank* contestants got to list one phone number that could be called for advice if needed during their pitch. I was that number, so the producers of the show called me that morning to instruct me on what would happen if they wanted to call me. They then called me 30 minutes before Tracey and Dani were scheduled to go in and told me to simply stay by my phone for the next couple of hours, or until I heard back from them that the pitch was finished.

"About an hour and a half later my phone rang. It was the producers telling me that they were patching Tracey through. The next thing I knew, I was talking to Tracey. She quickly explained Kevin's offer to me. She also explained that it was the only offer on the table. It threw me for a bit of a loop, since we hadn't taken into consideration the option of a royalty deal (we were the first royalty deal ever done on the show, so there was really no historical precedent). Luckily, I'm pretty good at doing math on the fly, so I quickly calculated what that royalty would mean to us in terms of cash flow and comparable percentage of equity. It was risky, but I felt like if we succeeded and grew like we wanted to, it would be a good deal for us. So I ultimately told her, "You're the one that's there. You've got a sense for the negotiation. Do what you think is right," said Scott.

Scott went on to explain, "To some, it may seem like I punted and offered no real advice. I see it differently. I felt like the structure of the deal wouldn't hurt us, so there was no wrong choice here. I had to trust Tracey and Dani at this point. They were the ones in the room. They were the ones who were hearing the feedback from the sharks. They were the ones doing the negotiating with Kevin. So ultimately, I had to defer to their gut feeling. Luckily for us, their gut was to accept the deal!"

Even after we spoke, Scott didn't know if we had accepted Kevin's offer. His last words to me were, "Do what you think is right." Awesome.

The good news was I felt like we were really prepared. We knew our numbers inside and out. We had a comeback for the commodity question that I knew was inevitable. I felt like we were in great shape. So why was I worried?

Well, the answer is simple. You see, you can be prepared and have all kinds of facts committed to memory all day long. The one thing I feared the most was out of my control. Would the five Sharks *like* the product?

I know you're thinking, "Shouldn't you have enough faith in your product so that isn't a worry?"

Yes. Absolutely. Don't get me wrong. I believe in and love our product all day long. But the thought that one of them could say, "This is awful" in front of eight million viewers was really scary. I don't care how confident in your product you are, no one wants to be bashed like that on national TV. And if you've ever watched the show, you know that happens.

Worry number two was that either Dani or myself were going to say something dumb, make a really stupid face, or any of the million other things I feared could go wrong.

I remember feeling really faint right before the doors swung open and we were to walk down the shark-lined hall. Dani was super keyed-up. I remember her nervously laughing and doing karate kicks before we had to take that *really* long walk. Her enthusiasm and sense of excitement helped calm me.

The doors opened, I took a deep breath, and we headed in. There was no turning back now.

At 23 years of age, as Dani walked through those same doors onto the *Shark Tank* set with her mom, she shared her thoughts: "Don't screw up. Don't say something stupid. Don't embarrass my mom in front of everybody. F*cking do it, own it, win it.

"Yet it was mostly like I didn't want to disappoint mom and when I don't want to disappoint her I put everything into it that I can. I also thought our company is being represented here and I worked my ass off for this company, so I better not blow it."

There are no reshoots or retakes on *Shark Tank*. It's do or die. We had rehearsed our pitch so many times before. I just prayed that my mouth would work once we were cued to start.

When our pitch was done, we were told not to speak to each other and were whisked away in a golf cart to another part of the Sony lot to record our exit interviews. It didn't air, but Dani had a complete meltdown during her exit interview.

Dani shared her thoughts about the exit interview. "So what you don't see is that I actually have a pretty epic meltdown. I actually started to cry and the producer was questioning us from the sideline, asking me 'Why are you crying?' I'm actually very surprised it didn't air. I pretty much started crying because I was thinking we made a deal with the devil. He's going to take all of our money and leave us. I'm literally sh*tting on Kevin and I feel bad, but I'm also just trying to express my concerns about it and I can feel my mom's eyes on me, saying stop crying, stop crying … I can't help it. This is really stressful and I don't want our company to fall apart, and this man to take all our money and run. Oh, it was very stressful.

"Fast forward several months later: Now that I have gotten to know Kevin, I can really appreciate all that he has done for us and we consider him part of the family. He is very supportive and takes very good care of us and I couldn't have asked for a better Shark to have picked us."

You see, before we left the Tank, Mark Cuban and Daymond John were riding Kevin and trash-talking, telling us that Kevin was going to bankrupt us and that we made a bad deal. I laughed it off because I knew they were just trash-talking, but poor Dani took it to heart. She was so upset and crying and the worst part was I couldn't even talk to her!

Dani said, "I didn't know that Mark and Daymond were just trash-talking. I thought they were serious. You know you're in front of a group of people that we don't know, but they know each other really well. So when they warned us not to accept the deal with Kevin, who are you going to believe? I didn't know who to believe. I was panicking. The anxiety of working so hard to start this business and there I was thinking this stranger is going to ruin it.

"I'm really glad it wasn't left up to me to decide. I trusted my mom even though I was in a panic."

That was a tough exit interview for sure.

After the exit interview, we were escorted back to our dressing room. Kevin's president of O'Leary Ventures, Alex (all the Sharks travel with key people from their organization for the show) stopped by our dressing room and introduced himself.

We had brought our bags along to the sound stage and we were taken to a lovely hotel at the airport so we could catch our flight home the next day. The producers and staff are very careful to keep any entrepreneurs who are pitching on the same day away from one another. They are very protective of the entrepreneurs and the emotions they may be experiencing, as well as maintaining the secrecy of the show's segments.

It takes a while for exactly what you've gone through to really sink in, even if you had a great experience and got an offer/deal like we did.

After we arrived at the airport hotel, we ate dinner at 4:00 that afternoon and spent the rest of the day lying in bed chatting and watching TV. I woke up around midnight and had my own cry. I honestly don't know why that happened, but I can tell you it was an extremely intense experience.

Shark Tank is one of those once-in-a-lifetime opportunities that if you're willing to take a chance, good or bad, it will be a game-changer for your business. I'm asked a lot if I'd do it again. Absolutely. I'd do it all again in a heartbeat.

The one thing I will advise if any of you are thinking about diving in – know your numbers. Nothing else is as important. Know your numbers. Also, go back and watch past episodes. Make notes on common-themed questions. You can't be too prepared for the Tank.

We were all really pleased with the final outcome. Mark Cuban actually ate four jars while we taped and everybody loved them. Yay!

The deal we struck with Kevin was quite simple. He gave us $75,000. In return, we were to pay him a dollar a jar/unit sold until the $75,000 was paid back in full. We would then enter the royalty portion of the deal, in which we would pay him 45 cents a jar for perpetuity. (Fun factoid: Kevin's $75,000 was paid back in full in just six short weeks.)

As you can imagine, we were amped. It was so hard to sleep that night. I was excited to return home. It was an exhilarating but long five days. Little did I know that the real work was about to begin!

The World, Post-*Shark Tank*

After a deal is struck on *Shark Tank* and an agreement is reached, the Sharks do their due diligence on you. Financials, CORI checks, tax returns, bank statements; you name it, it's checked and double-checked. Contracts are drawn and a plan to implement execution is established.

Alex traveled from Toronto, where Kevin is based, to visit our Cohasset facility. To this day I'm convinced it was to check and make sure we were who we said we were. And I get it. When you're standing on that carpet in front of the Sharks, it's easy to say anything. But if you want a deal, you had best tell the truth, otherwise everything will fall apart during your due diligence. The Sharks are wealthy for a reason and being stupid isn't one of them.

One of our biggest concerns over the course of the next few months was execution. We were hopeful that at some point during Season Four we were going to air and the "*Shark Tank* Effect" was going to hit. We knew this was going to be a huge opportunity and we wanted to be 100 per cent prepared.

Of course, that's completely ridiculous when you think about it. No one has any way of knowing what to expect that night or during the subsequent days as far as a sales number goes. But you do need to be ready. It's like a first-time expectant mother. You don't really know what to expect, but you know something's coming!

We had been interviewing commercial bakeries around the Boston area in the hopes of finding someone who would bake our recipes our way. Yeah. Easier said than done. Never mind the fact that they would have to assemble and pack for shipping. This was not going to be a piece of cake (sorry).

It took some time, but we finally found a fit for our product – and just in time. Kevin had wrangled a spot on *Good Morning America's* "Shark Tank Steals and Deals." I was in a panic, because we hadn't aired yet. Remember the five-million-dollar NDA? But Kevin convinced us it was okay with the show execs and in November of 2012 we hit the air.

In hindsight, it was a great pre-*Shark Tank* air test. We got to experience a small bump, see how the website fared, and fix any problems we found within our systems.

After a few bumps, we ended up doing okay and buckled down to prepare for the airing of the show.

We also had the extremely rare opportunity to open up a small 125 sq. ft. shop in Boston's Faneuil Hall. The rent was crazy high, but we knew that it would be a huge marketing opportunity for us. With so many vacationers passing through there, able to try our product, we had a ready-made audience who hopefully would "bring" us home and continue to order online. We signed the lease and readied ourselves to open May 1, 2013.

After months of waiting and false alarms with air dates, we were finally scheduled in ABC's lineup. We aired at the end of April 2013. When we pitched the Sharks, we had $150,000 worth of sales with a projection to do about $320,000 that year. The five days following our *Shark Tank* air, we did $250,000 in sales. In five days! Talk about a wave!

I'm still not sure how we did it, but we managed to get everything out the door on time.

We quickly learned the areas of our business that needed to be improved upon on, like customer service. We simply didn't have enough bodies or phone lines at the time to accommodate the traffic. Epic fail with a lesson learned.

It was scary and overwhelming and simply amazing. The morning after *Shark Tank* we had thousands of e-mails. It took over a week for the phone to stop ringing incessantly and for us to plow through our voicemails. We were tired, but so happy and most importantly, really proud of ourselves. We pulled together, buckled down and made magic happen with a little bit of help from an amazing show called *Shark Tank* and a man they call Mr. Wonderful.

CHAPTER 8

THE KEVIN O'LEARY FACTOR

Is Kevin O'Leary Really Mr. Wonderful?

As you can imagine, we are invited to do a fair amount of public speaking. My favorite part, besides meeting so many awesome people, is when we have our Q & A segment.

Invariably one question always arises: "What is it like working with Kevin O'Leary? Is he really Mr. Wonderful?"

I'm here to tell you, yes he is. Kevin is fabulous to work with and he is wonderful.

When we first consummated our deal and then subsequently paid Kevin back, I wasn't sure how involved he was going to be from that point forward. After all, his end of the deal was done and he was paid in full ($75,000 paid back in full in six weeks).

I have to say, I was a bit sad thinking that may be the last of him, but to my pleasant surprise it was really just the beginning!

I'm happy to report that our investor, mentor, and friend is an active and very big part of Wicked Good. He is interested and will give sound, honest advice when asked, but leaves the decision-making up to Dani, Scott, and me.

He has stated many times that he respects us as a family business and that as such, we need to be the ultimate decision-makers. That being said, he is never more than an e-mail, text or phone call away. We have conversations weekly and are also fortunate enough to have the time and attention of O'Leary Ventures and the talent that works tirelessly with him.

He's a very personable, funny and (yes) warm man who is soft-spoken and binary. With Kevin there is no gray area. He's also a ton of fun to party with.

As of this writing, it's been two and a half years now that we've been part of the O'Leary fold and there's not a day that goes by that we're not grateful for all of the things he has done for us and included us to be a part of.

We're looking forward to many, many years ahead with our charismatic and often "to the point" partner.

Together we have built a national brand.

In closing, all I can say is this;

Kevin, we love and respect you
and are so happy that you have become
such an important part
of our Wicked Good family.
Thank you.
Here's to many more
"wonderful" years together.
~ T xo ~

One of the Many Advantages
of Knowing Mr. Wonderful
The Profit

May 2014. It was a beautiful day, Dani's birthday to be exact, and we were at the Taj Hotel in Boston waiting for Kevin to show up. We had a breakfast meeting scheduled along with a taping of a local ABC affiliate show called *Chronicle*.

I'm always asked what Kevin is like to work with. This question always makes me smile. To know Kevin O'Leary is to love him. Truly.

Kevin is really soft-spoken, generous of his time, and a whole lot of fun. He loves *Shark Tank* and what it has done, not only for reality television, but for people like Dani, Scott, and me. He has witnessed time and time again how it can truly change people's lives. He's passionate about photography and music. He's an amazing guitarist. He loves his family and he loves that we make him more money.

We're so blessed to have been paired with him. Dani no longer fears that he's going to ruin us (thanks, Mark and Daymond, for that…). He's as committed to us as we are to him. He's very accessible, sensible, and will always be a part of our Wicked Good family.

Have you ever wondered if lightning strikes the same place twice? I'm here to tell you it can and it does.

While catching up and enjoying a lovely breakfast, Kevin mentioned in passing that a CNBC TV personality named Marcus had been inquiring about us. He wanted Kevin to introduce us. Scott and I both stopped mid-chew. I said to Kevin, "Who did you say?"

He looked at me and said, "Marcus."

I replied with, "Lemonis?" Yup. Marcus Lemonis knew of our business and wanted an introduction. I felt like I might faint.

Marcus owns a number of food-related businesses and had recently been credited with bailing out the recently bankrupted cupcake shop, Crumbs.

Scott and I had just recently stumbled across Marcus' show, *The Profit*, on CNBC and were immediately hooked. (It's a great show. I strongly recommend you watch.)

A conference call was arranged and we met Marcus via the phone. We initially chatted about using one of his commercial kitchens located in Chicago to do some of our distribution.

The quality I most liked about Marcus was his genuine interest, not only in our company, but his concern for us as the business owners. I immediately felt comfortable and liked him instantly.

As our relationship has grown, we've had the opportunity to really get to know and understand Marcus. People, process, and product; these are his core values and as such have contributed to making him the very successful businessman he is (as well as a lovely human being).

As mentioned earlier, Marcus had recently acquired the newly bankrupt Crumbs Bake Shop. Crumbs enjoyed a meteoric rise to fame as the first cupcake shop to be publicly traded. His plan was to build a one-stop bake shop featuring the food-related businesses in his portfolio, of which Wicked Good Bake Shop is one.

We have entered a strategic partnership with Marcus and are excited about the endless possibilities this means for us and all of the other wonderful businesses he's a part of. He dreams big and like Kevin is completely accessible. Imagine that. Never did I ever dream any of this would happen for us! But it did.

And all because I took a chance and applied to *Shark Tank*. Remember ... what did I have to lose? And the next time you have a great idea, ask yourself, what do you have to lose by following your dream?

www.WickedGoodCupcakes.com

CHAPTER 9

DAILY CHALLENGES AND
SECRETS TO GROWING A BUSINESS

Your New Business, or as We Say in Boston...
Getting Stahted

I f you've read all this and are still feeling confident that you can do this thing, then allow me to share with you the ups and downs we have experienced over the past four very short years. Remember that neither Dani nor myself are MBAs. As a matter of fact, neither of us finished college. We didn't have a million dollars when we started our company. We started with a $30,000 loan from my husband's 401K.

So lay those fears to rest and repeat after me:

I do not need an MBA to succeed.

I also don't need tons of cash.

What you do require is passion, drive, and the ability to pick yourself up and dust yourself off when the going gets tough. Because invariably it will. I hope by sharing, I can help prevent you from making some of the mistakes we made when we first started. (Did I mention my zero business background?)

Starting your own business is the toughest and at the same time the most exciting and terrifying endeavor you will ever experience. But if you have the stomach for it, I highly recommend giving it a shot. If I had a dollar for every person I've met who has said to me, "I wish I tried" or "I wish I had done something of my own" I wouldn't need to have a business at all. Seriously. Don't be that person who lives with regret. You never know how high you'll fly unless you spread your wings and make the leap off that ledge.

When Dani and I finally made that decision to go for it, we knew that at the very least, the first thing we needed was a name for our biz.

Our name, Wicked Good Cupcakes, is a federally registered trademark. This was not an accident. Once we were emotionally committed to our business, I began to dream. I dreamed of the size of our company and in my mind's eye I watched it grow. I was convinced we would be a national brand, although at that point I had no idea how that would happen.

People who take risks and put themselves out there are generally people who have an innate feeling that they're going to make it. I've always had a voice in my head that told me that I was destined to do something big.

I'd be willing to bet that a lot of you have had this same experience. But most of us, myself included until very recently, never wanted to share this intense, emotional feeling with others because we fear ridicule or we're afraid people will take such a statement the wrong, boastful kind of way. Remember dear friends, there is nothing wrong with having confidence and a belief in one's self. It is truly a gift from a higher power to have such strong and supportive confidence in one's self from within.

And no, you don't have to tell the world you have this self-knowledge, but you do need to act upon it. Not everyone will have the courage or the belief in themselves to be able to strike out and start something big. It's not easy. There are many days when I question, "What am I doing?" or say, "This is hard." But at the end of the day when I go to bed and lie quietly with my thoughts, I somehow seem to *know* that I can do this. That I should do this. I know I can build a business and make something from nothing. Embrace and believe these thoughts if you have them. Allow them to give you courage and confidence. That's why they're there in the first place.

Now Back to the Business of Your Trademark

I knew if we were going to have a large presence/brand that eventually lawyers would need to be involved. I wanted everything neat and tidy from the beginning. So registering our name just seemed like the obvious thing to do. (I will add the disclaimer now, that I am *not* an attorney and *strongly* recommend that you hire one to help with this process!)

The first step we took was to write down a huge list of potential business name candidates. We had maybe 75 names on a list by the time our little brains were exhausted of any other ideas. The next thing we needed to figure out was, is the name we like already in use? The approach we took was simple. We did Google searches to find companies, as well as domain name searches on domain acquisition sites. If someone had a website under that name, we immediately crossed it off the list. Remember, a domain may be spoken for, but may not be in use at this time. If someone is sitting on a name that you love, you may want to contact that "owner" and see if you can negotiate a sale.

In retrospect, Wicked Good should have been one of the first potential names on our list! For those of you not fortunate enough to have been born a Bostonian, you may not understand the use of the word "wicked." Wicked is used as an adjective in these parts. We say things like wicked smart, wicked tired, wicked old … you get the drift. I don't know how or why that name was available, but I'm mighty glad (wicked happy) that it was!

On a humorous note, be sure to check and see if there are any double-entendres associated with the name you 'simply must have.' I loved the name Pink Monkey Bakery. That was, until my husband pointed out that if I had done my search online like I should have, I would have found out that Pink Monkey was the name of a strip club. Yup. Not the adorable pink cartoon monkeys I had envisioned. That oversight could have been a really stupid, albeit funny, mistake.

Here is where I will again *strongly* urge you to do your homework. Should you fall in love with a name and find it's already in use, but decide to use it anyway, you are setting yourself up to experience a whole world of hurt. Infringing on someone's trademarked name is a federal offense punishable by many nasty fines and penalties such as treble damages, an immediate cease and desist, which will also include tearing down your website, and potential jail time. If you're having trouble sleeping nights, I recommend reading up on trademarks and patents here: http://www.uspto.gov/trademarks/basics/BasicFacts.pdf

Remember this. Not only are you breaking the law, but you're taking something somebody else already has a legitimate claim to. That's just plain old bad kismet, in my opinion. There were several names that

I was disappointed to find were already spoken for, but at the end of the day there is always going to be a name for your business if you put your mind to it. And it will be all yours.

Once you find a name and there's no website domain registered using that name, do yourself a favor and check on the government's patent and trademark website. If you don't feel confident searching yourself, this may be the point where you need to engage a good IP (intellectual property) attorney.

Your IP attorney will be able to search names and then give you incredibly important advice as to how to proceed. If no one has registered that name and you can't find a domain in use, claim that name as your own. Go to http://www.top10domainregistration.com and check out the different companies where you can register your new business name.

To trademark your name requires legal advice from a competent IP attorney. You could go to the government's site and do it yourself at http://www.uspto.gov/trademarks/basics/howtofile.jsp or legalzoom. com. I will caution you that unless you're a stickler for detail and read everything five times before you sign on the dotted line, I suggest you hire a professional. Mistakes in the application process can cost you dearly in the form of time and money. If and when in doubt, please call your attorney!

Once you have your name registered, your work doesn't end there. You must be vigilant and do searches online to be certain no one else is benefiting from your hard work by infringing upon your federally-registered and trademarked name.

We once had a bakery in New Hampshire start using our name. I wasn't aware until our customers asked us why we had a second Facebook page. And to make matters worse, the customers were all commenting on how bad the New Hampshire product looked. Imagine my horror when I found the fraudulent page and saw what was being represented as our work.

Scott and I even drove to the bakery in question to check them out ourselves. I can't believe the anger and feeling of sheer violation I felt seeing our company's name on their sign. I may have thrown up. I can't remember. It was like a bad dream.

When we went into the bakery I kept my mouth shut. If you knew me, you'd be impressed. I let my husband do the talking.

He made some small talk while I stood there silently fuming. The owner, whose name was also Tracey, (could it get any f*cking worse?) chatted back.

Then Scott dropped the question. "Hey did you know that a company down in Massachusetts where we come from is also called Wicked Good Cupcakes?" Her mood suddenly changed. "Yeah, I know," was the response.

Scott, sensing my wrath, pushed a bit more. He told this Tracey that he was an IP attorney and that what they were doing was actually against the law. She responded by saying she was in New Hampshire and it didn't matter. Scott told her it in fact did. Trademarks are federal/national.

She said she didn't care. I had to leave. We contacted our IP attorney when we returned home that afternoon.

After phone calls and letters from our IP attorney, these women finally changed the name of their business before we took them to court. I'm usually not the first to run to court with an issue, but protecting my business was and always will be the exception. I will go to any length that it takes to protect our business and our reputation. Remember, at the end of the day your reputation is all you have. You don't need a "poser" destroying what you've worked so hard to build. Protect your business at any and all costs. Don't allow squatters to hang out on your brand! Really!

Whew. I always get all fired up when it comes to this subject. Onward.

Congratulations! You now have a business and your business has a name. Good for you.

The Mission Statement

Before I sat down to work with Scott and Dani on our business plan, I felt it was important to define who we were and who we wanted to be. We needed to write a mission statement. Wikipedia defines a mission statement as this: "A Mission Statement is a statement of the purpose of a company, organization, or person, its reason for existing. The mission statement should guide the actions of the organization, spell out its overall goal, provide a path, and guide decision-making."

Sounds easy, right? In theory it should be. You don't want to pen the Declaration of Independence. Your mission statement should be relevant and it should be brief. You must clearly convey to yourself, your employees, and the customers you hope to have, your vision either long-term or short-term while keeping it short and sweet.

Check out other companies that you admire. Read their mission statements and if they're a business you have patronized, think about whether or not they've really been true to their mission statements. This will force you to think about your baby business and how you'd like it to run and be perceived. Remember, your customer's perception is *your* reality. A brilliant statement indeed.

Once you have inked that mission statement, keep a copy of it where you will see it every day. Print it out and stick copies on your bathroom mirror, on your fridge, even on the dashboard of your car. Your company's mission statement is your mantra, your belief system. It's your business. Embrace it, share it with your employees, and revisit it often no matter how big and or successful you become.

You now have your mission statement as your company's moral compass. Now you need a timeline.

Your Business Timeline

A timeline is the next step in making your business a reality. Without that ticking clock, it's much too easy to keep putting off the tasks that need to be done in order to open your doors.

This task can be really hard for many entrepreneurs. It's your committal. And by the way, a date set can always be changed if necessary. But I've found in speaking with a number of would-be business owners that even with the knowledge the date can change doesn't lessen the power behind having a timeline.

So you've picked your date. May 20th of this year. Now work backwards. Figure out the date you need to have a lease secured, inspections done, product ordered, and employees hired. Make lists. Make lists of lists and be sure that you have all of the legal obligations in place that you need to open. Make sure licenses, inspections, and insurances are done. Wireless, registers, and phones all need dates to be up and running by. And always assume things will take longer to schedule and execute than you anticipate. You will be at the mercy of many people's schedules. Plan accordingly. Don't leave *anything* to the last minute or you will be sorry.

Use your timeline as the push you need to power through the days that are scary or hard. It will give you focus and keep you on track. And speaking of keeping you on track ...

Your Business Plan

Now comes the hard part; at least it was for me. Your business plan. You need to write the dreaded business plan. In reality, it's a great way to organize your thoughts and put an action plan into place. It's also a really good benchmark as your business grows. It's important to note that writing a business plan is not always a one-shot deal. You may find you have to write and rewrite this plan again and again as your business morphs into the company it's supposed to be.

If I were to show you our original business plan, you might not know it's the same business we operate today. When we started, we weren't producing our cupcake jars. We opened as a small retail bakery that created custom cakes and cupcakes. Our foray into cupcakes in mason jars was born out of necessity, because we had a website and an online presence and we were constantly being asked if we could ship our product.

So as you can imagine, our original business plan was no longer relevant. And we now became a company that shipped product in mason jars.

It's very important to note how our business changed so organically. The differentiator that we had developed came to us through a need to solve a problem. Cupcakes on their own don't ship well. But put them in an airtight container and boom, shipping problem solved, we could reach more customers and our cupcakes stayed fresher longer! Boom! A shipping dream, more customer reach, and a product that stayed fresher longer.

We allowed our business to take the direction it needed to take by allowing it to show us the direction we should head in. It's fun to see where we've grown and really interesting to look at how much our business plan has changed. And yes, I still apologize to Scott when I think about the opportunity we could have missed, all because I thought he was a big dummy.

You may feel the need to revisit your existing business plan if your find that your company has gone through tremendous growth or a change in your product line. At this point the ball is in your court. If you need to rewrite it to help keep yourself focused and on track, then do so. If not, don't. But always maintain strict awareness of any changes to the original plan as your expenses, need for more or less labor, and growth strategy may be affecting your bottom line. Frequent adjustments and a watchful eye help keep your financial house in order.

If you're anything like me, the thought of a business plan is daunting. I knew I had no idea how to write one, so I did some research online and found one of the most amazing *free* resources available to any would-be start up. Your local chapter of SCORE.

Here's a link to SCORE's website. https://www.score.org/.

In a nutshell, SCORE works like this. You make an appointment with your local chapter and they assign retired business professionals who fit your need and business acumen. You all agree to a time each week to meet. And that's it. Simple.

Every Tuesday at 9:00 a.m. I would drive to the SCORE office and sit down with three lovely, older men who would offer guidance and advice and point out some important challenges and tasks that needed to be addressed. We talked at length about insurance needed, equipment, employees, taxes, certifications, and licenses. And while I only went to six sessions, I took away a lot of insight and felt like I could at least begin to tackle the writing of my business plan.

We were fortunate that we didn't need money to start out on our journey into the business world, but if we had, a business plan would have been vital. No bank or investor will give you one millisecond of their time if you don't have a proper business plan. No ifs, ands, or buts. It's important to note that an investor of any sort will not be willing to hand over even one red cent if he or she has no confidence in you or your business plan. If you find you're struggling with penning this important document, you may want to hire someone to help. It's money well spent. There are lots of students in business school who could use some pocket money. Investigate any and all avenues in regards to finding assistance when it comes to writing your business plan. Your company depends on it!

Our Recipe for Success

I look at our business plan as if it is a recipe. Adding to the recipe or plan are your key ingredients. And then the baking instructions.

Our key ingredients are:

1) Know your numbers/measurements. You can't bake anything that'll be worth eating if the measurements or numbers aren't correct. Take your time and make sure the numbers work. If they don't, make the necessary adjustments or your business won't work.

2) Know the order in which you combine your ingredients. Organization of your systems, finances, and how much time/money you devote to each is critical. If you're paying too much attention to one aspect of your business while not involving/combining other aspects, you'll have a business that won't set up like a good mix should.

3) Timing. Don't spend too little time on an area you may not like working on but must, or put too much time into an area that's not going to give you a good return. Timing is everything. Use your mental timer. Be aware of wasted time. Opportunities, growth, and success all require time and perfect timing (there *is* a difference!). It's how you monitor this time that determines whether your recipe/plan will be a success or a flop.

Have a plan and know your numbers. Mr. Wonderful would be so proud of you.

"You Can't be Afraid to Kill Your Darlings"

Our jars are now our mainstay product. We no longer bake and sell regular cupcakes. We've added new items to our repertoire, all while carefully monitoring what works and what doesn't.

We've had tons of success growing our corporate customer business simply by customizing the lid and jar labels with corporate branding. Our corporate customers can add a note or card in branded packages, making these jars the perfect gift at holiday time or for marketing purposes.

Event planners love us because we offer people planning weddings, bar mitzvahs, graduations, birthdays, etc., the opportunity to have personalized favors! Bingo.

Where we've run into difficulty innovating new product is in the cost of shipping a perishable product.

As we have grown, we developed a line of delicious cheesecakes baked in mason jars, but recently discontinued the line (for now) because the cost to the consumer to ship these was so prohibitive. Overnight shipping with dry ice is a killer and trust me, at this point we get very good rates from UPS!

One of the phrases I learned from my brief stint as a screenwriter was, "You can't be afraid to kill your darlings." In other words, be prepared to get rid of what isn't working, even if you're attached to it.

This was true of me and the cheesecake. We had rave reviews about this product, but few sales. Why? Because people didn't want to pay the shipping costs. It was just that simple.

It was hard for me to let go of this product for a few reasons. Reason number one, we didn't have a lot of other products. If you're not innovating and giving people new products and other options, you are going to inadvertently send them elsewhere because people don't always want to send the same thing. This is a huge fear of mine.

The other reason I didn't want to kill this product was because it was really good. Unfortunately, the cost of keeping dry ice and packaging on hand for a product that you're not selling a whole lot of isn't smart. For the few sales, you're actually spending more on inventory and space. Ugh.

I'm hopeful that someday down the road we can resurrect these yummy jars, but until such time we've had to "take the cheesecake out behind the barn and shoot it" as Kevin O'Leary would say. Sigh. Just another casualty of a perishable product and small margins. The food industry is so tough.

It's definitely not for the faint of heart.

I spend a great deal of time researching trends in the dessert, baking, and food industry, as well as other industries.

I test bake in my free time and then ask people to try and (honestly) rate what they think about the new product.

Sometime flavors are a huge hit, like our Mr. Wonderful's Cookie Butter, and sometimes they're a miss, like our chocolate-and-orange-flavored jar.

By keeping statistics and by obtaining valuable customer feedback we can quickly kill a flavor that's proving to be a dog while ramping up for a flavor that takes off.

We hardly ever do short runs of a flavor, because the cost to do the R & D can prove to be more than the sales will return. That being said, we've been very lucky with our seasonals. We usually feature four flavors that are seasonal and usually three are very popular out of the four. This info gives us what we need in order to try a new seasonal flavor along with the standbys that our customers wait for. We also have extended the amount of time seasonal flavors are available in order to take advantage of sales. Pumpkin is the perfect example. Most people introduce pumpkin the end of August. We were waiting and releasing our pumpkin in October. That was really much too late. We were losing out on the excitement/sales that launching a new flavor brings with it. By the end of fall, everyone is pretty much pumpkined-out. But by releasing this popular jar flavor earlier, we have experienced greater returns because people are swept up in the excitement/novelty of a new flavor. Basically, if you aren't offering that flavor when demand is great, your customers will go elsewhere and nobody in business wants that to happen! It's always about the customer; your goal is to serve your customers when and where they want your products. Do that and you can be successful; don't do that and you are going to fail.

Finding the Time to Just Be…

It's no secret that we all lead busy lives. Between family, work, and social commitments it sometimes feels as though we need to schedule time just to breathe.

I'm guilty of this. If I'm not at work, I'm thinking about work.

I used to have horses and would ride regularly, but when Wicked Good started, that hobby ended. I missed having that time to unwind and "just be." Enter my husband and the best Valentine's Day gift ever: my very first drum kit.

That's right, I play the drums. Scott bought the kit for me as a way to distract, unleash, and entertain the part of me that needed a creative outlet. I was immediately hooked.

My drums have a place of honor in our cellar. I can venture down whenever I want and wail away to my heart's content. I take lessons when my schedule permits. I watch instructional videos on YouTube, but mostly I play along with my favorite band and get lost in the world that music has to offer.

I'm not great, but I'm also not that bad. The important thing is I'm having fun, I'm giving myself much needed "me time," and I'm creating a sound that's unique to me.

I invite you to find that something that gives you a break, whether it be mountain biking, kick boxing, or the violin.

We make sure to take the time to nourish our bodies. Remember, it's equally important to take the time to nourish your soul.

CHAPTER 10

RUNNING A NATIONAL BRAND
IN YOUR 20s

Butcher, Baker, Candlestick Maker.
What Business(es) are You in?

If I were to ask you what business you were in, what would you say?

This probably sounds very obvious to you, but think about it. What business are you really in? You are a knitter of nose warmers. Knit wear. Is that it? Really think about this for a minute. Okay, okay. Let me shed some light. Maybe this will help.

Take Wicked Good Cupcakes, for example. What business do you think we're in? Most of you have probably said the words "cupcakes," "bakery," or "baked goods." You get my drift. Well, it might surprise you to know that this is not entirely correct. Cupcakes are simply one of our products. In reality, we are in three different businesses. Technology, distribution, and gifting.

We have a strong online presence with a robust e-commerce engine. Seventy-five per cent of our business comes from online sales. These sales need to be tracked, integrated with our distribution and inventory channels, and available to our customer service department in order to aid our customers.

Our inventory and supply chains also depend heavily on the use of technology. Tracking the number of boxes, jars, spoons, cards, labels, and everything else really helps us know what product we need in stock and helps our forecasting for the next day, month, and year.

If we see that we're up 40 per cent from last year, we know we need to check what sales were each day we were open last year in order to make an educated decision as to how much product to bake and what to order for inventory based on hard numbers. Without spreadsheets and tracking online orders this job would be crazy hard. Impossible, really. We apply the same principals with our brick-and-mortar shops.

Faneuil Hall attracts more than 18 million visitors per year and is listed as one of the top 10 most-visited tourist sites in the world. As a result, you can imagine the influx of customers and how sales can vary based on the time of year, economic climate (this affects vacationers) and even the weather on any given day.

I can't remember what I ate for dinner the night before, never mind what we sold or even what the weather was like on December 18th of 2012. Tracking this data and the inventory management along with the website and our e-commerce puts us squarely in the technology business.

My husband, Scott, came on board full-time in January, 2014. His responsibilities involve a host of tech-related duties which include SEO, online security, knowing all of the laws and regulations surrounding selling online, as well as how to change and manage website content. All of that and more. We are a tech company. Who knew?

Technology Should be Your Friend

S cott shared his insights surrounding technology. "If you ask someone what business we're in, they would probably answer 'cupcakes' or 'baked goods.' If you asked me, I would answer 'customer service,' 'shipping and distribution,' and 'technology.' Our product may be baked goods, but without those other three business units running well and efficiently, we would ultimately fail," said Scott.

"Today's consumer is so technology-driven that you have to be able to keep up. Luckily for us, my background allowed us to do what a lot of other small start-ups wouldn't have been able to do without significant investment.

"The importance of technology cannot be understated. We were the first website in the history of *Shark Tank* (or so we were told) that didn't crash during airing. I cannot stress how important this is. You only get this opportunity once and not capitalizing on it could have been devastating.

"And it doesn't stop there. Having systems in place to manage packaging inventory, order fulfillment, customer engagement, etc., all play a huge part in our success. When you're shipping 6,000 packages out in a day, you have to have efficient systems to manage and track all of that.

"The other point to stress is how technology should be invisible to your customers and help them in the process of purchasing with you.

Just putting up a website isn't enough. How you present the information and how you manage the check-out process can mean the difference between a sale and a lost customer. For example, do you know that depending on who you talk to, roughly three out of four consumers who put an item in their shopping cart never actually buy it (reference: http://listrak.com/ecommerce-marketing-automation/channels/email/shopping-cart-abandonment-index.aspx)? That's a pretty staggering number. There are many reasons why this happens, but the point is, we've invested tremendous time and effort into making the purchase process as seamless and easy as possible for our customers. The result, instead of a cart abandonment rate of 75 per cent (industry average), ours is only 45 per cent.

"We've consistently maintained conversion rates well above industry standards because of the amount of importance we've placed on technology. At the end of the day, this means more sales for us. So now you understand why I say we're really a technology company," said Scott.

Because a majority of our business is done online, we need a way to get that product to our customers. We ship to all 50 states in the U.S. and rarely does a month pass that we don't ship at least one package to each state.

We also have the unique challenge that we ship a perishable product. As such, we require that products arrive at the customer's location within three consecutive days. Because of this, we're also in the distribution business. We need to know everything about how our product gets safely from point A to point B.

We are vigilant at monitoring shipping rates, weeding through those painfully long UPS bills, knowing how much a package weighs just by virtue of looking at it and feeling it, how long ground vs. next day air vs. next day air saver take to any given state on any given day. We have our UPS rep on speed dial and we know the weather in all parts of the country. All of this helps us to plan our shipping accordingly.

We know how many jars ship bulk in a certain size box. We know how to wrap and pack product in order to fit the same number of jars in said box ... see where this is going? Distribution. Another business we need to be very well versed in.

Lastly, we sell a product that is sent as a gift the majority of the time. This makes us a gifting business. We need to constantly add to, or change up our online selection and to follow trends in the gifting world as well as the gourmet food industry. We may have started with cupcakes, but it can't stop there. Not if we want repeat business.

One of my (many) tasks is to be on top of trends, whether it be in food/tastes, colors, or fashion.

It is my job to know what trends are hot and what are not. That knowledge also helps with new product development (another subject for later).

Of course, our product is important. Without it, we have no basis for a business. But it's just that – a product. Growing a successful business requires understanding and becoming experts in these other areas.

I think it's safe to say that as a business owner you're going to find yourself working less and less with your passion (for me it was baking and decorating) and spending more energy working on everything else. That's why taking the much-needed focus and time to learn every single aspect of your business is vital to your company's success and growth. You don't need to be an expert in every field, but you do need to understand the inner workings that make up your business.

Take the time to figure out what business(es) you're really in and watch your business boom!

Social Media: Friend or Foe?

D ani is very involved in the social media side of Wicked Good Cupcakes. She shared her thoughts on how social media can be a double-edged sword. "To be honest, I learned that people are very brave and can be very mean-spirited when they are hiding behind a keyboard. A lot of the things that people said just made me wonder, why would you even think that? Like some things were kind of sh*tty when they were directed towards my mom or the family, which was just really awful, but after a month of just getting these stupid e-mails, I was done and really didn't care anymore, and to this day I still don't care.

"I don't follow social media as closely as some people do. If I know it's going to upset me, I don't even look at it. The one thing I can't stand is lying and it sucks because as an owner, I can't really defend myself without looking like I'm a giant dick. It's not fair, because you may be calling me out about something you don't even know about and if I even try to protect myself or anyone else, I look like the bad guy. So I don't even bother. On my personal Facebook page, I keep that very private.

"The hardest thing, I guess, was my mom reading the e-mails at first, because she would cry. She would cry a lot, because she thought one person would ruin our business. I finally would say to her, do you know how many people are actually here in the United States that don't give a sh*t, me included? So, I just learned quickly that people sometimes hate on you and no matter what you do, you can be Mother Teresa and unhappy people are still going to sh*t on you. One thing I've found to help my mom through all of this stuff was Jimmy Kimmel. He does a thing called "Mean Tweets" with all the celebrities who got mean tweets from these random people all over the country. I wanted to show her that you could be a movie star and people are still going to diss you. It happens all the time with everyone.

"Social media is a forum that seems to attract bullies. You just have to grow a thick skin and you just have to ignore it. I mean, it's easier to say than do, but you just have to get over the fact that you're not going to please everybody and there are going to be unhappy people who are just looking for someone to dump on. Even if you give them everything they say they want, more than half the time they still won't like you and that's fine. No one has to revolve their life around these negative people. I obviously have better, positive people in my life and that's just how I have to deal with it. Social media is always going to be there and there is always going to be someone reaching out to try and ruin your day, but that's just when you really have to ignore it."

You Don't Know it All ...
and That's Okay

Ignorance was bliss for a while, anyway. Then I realized I didn't know it all. As a Type A personality, control freak, and micro-manager, letting go of any part of our business was nothing short of sheer torture for me. I had myself convinced that no one could decorate as well as me. No one could order as efficiently as me. No one would ever be able to do anything that I could do nearly as well as me.

Boy, was I ever wrong. Not only did I have to admit to myself that I couldn't physically do everything, but I just wasn't good at everything. Ouch! And so, with that being said, I admit it: I don't know it all.

Listen up all of you Type As out there. Once you hear yourself say these magic words, "I don't know everything," and even better, "I can't do it all myself," you will not only increase the bottom line of your business, but you might even find yourself breathing a huge sigh of relief.

Now you'll actually be able to get out of your own way and bring in the much smarter/needed help that you need. It's been proven time and time again that once a business owner lets go of the choke-hold they have on their own company, the faster, stronger, and healthier it grows. Surround yourself with those who know more than you. Not only will they lift that heavy burden off your shoulders, but they'll also make you and your business look really good! And who doesn't want to look good?

When we first started out in the new commercial shop, neither Dani nor I had any clue as to how to order in bulk. Remember we had been shopping at the local wholesale club, which was hardly the way we needed to be purchasing goods in our "real" day-to-day biz.

I called our food distributor and set up a meeting with a sales rep. I remember our first meeting like yesterday. Topher, our fabulous rep, showed up with his note pad, sat down with me and after some exchanged pleasantries he asked what I wanted to order.

I looked him square in the eye and without missing a beat responded with, "I don't know." He looked up from his pad and said, "Excuse me?"

I replied calmly, "Not only do I not know what I want, I have no idea what I need." He smiled, rolled up his sleeves, and said, "Let's begin here. What are you baking?" And from there, we managed to struggle through our very first order together.

Fast forward. Topher and I have remained really good friends. We still laugh about that first day. If I had tried to order without knowing how, I could have cost us hundreds of dollars in wasted product. That's real money that we just didn't have to spare, never mind stupidly lose.

I think it's important to always remember that we can all learn something from someone else. My employees are a wealth of knowledge for me, not only in the baking sense, but also in regards to the world at large. Our employees are a unique blend of ages, socio-economic statuses, and diverse interests.

By asking people what's going on in their world, you're gaining valuable insight into the minds of different consumers.

Think about how wonderful it is to know what a twenty-something, thirty-something, forty- and fifty-somethings are interested in, what they watch on TV, what they read about, and what they enjoy doing in their spare time. This is valuable marketing information if you're willing to really listen.

Take millennials, for example. Millennial college students (without full-time jobs) spend $784 a month on discretionary expenses, especially food and entertainment, according to the Mooslyvania Marketing Agency. Millennials are also notoriously loyal to companies who support charities near and dear to them (look at Tom's Shoes and Friends of Toms).

According to an interesting article in businessnewsdaily.com, the vast differences between Gen X (people born between 1964-1977) purchasers and Gen Y (people born between 1978-1998) purchasers makes it close to impossible to market to both groups successfully, simultaneously.

"Generation X is very motivated to search for purchase-related information and is adept at searching. Generation Xers tend to use information not as a point of pride, but as assurance that they are not being taken advantage of by marketers and are getting the best deal possible," said Nelson Barber, associate professor of hospitality management at the University of New Hampshire, who contributed to the article. "Generation Y selects and consumes products that help them achieve their goals of blending in with the crowd or a certain group; thus, they are influenced by the need to conform in order to be liked and accepted by them," states Barber.

This information, when gathered and used properly, can help you strategize and reach your best potential customer without wasting precious advertising dollars by merely spending blindly.

Get to know all of those who exist in the world around you. I can't possibly stress this enough.

If you can infiltrate different groups by learning about spending habits and what each age's specific needs/wants are, you've cracked a major marketing code. This is what marketing companies spend millions to do.

Not only that, you're taking the time to get to know the people who work with you and those who are purchasing your product or using your service.

Technology is another area that confounds me on a daily basis. At this point I can navigate around, send e-mails, and handle social media, but when it comes to advising or explaining how we do what we do online, I gratefully hand the reins over to Scott.

It was tough to put my pride in my pocket and ask for help, but in the long run I did what was best for our company. By admitting that I didn't know it all, I freed up my tiny brain in order to be able to do necessary research that was vital to my business's direction and growth.

I learned to ask, research, listen, and learn.

And now I know how to order ingredients for the shop. Imagine that.

Employees. Yup, You Need 'Em.

You have acknowledged to the world that you do not know it all. Sooooo, now what?

Well, you need to surround yourself with those who do. That means hiring employees.

Let the games begin.

How many times have you been in a restaurant and have had an outstanding waiter or waitress. It's lovely, isn't it? Why, you can't wait to tip them and show them just how much you appreciated the attention that was paid to you and your party. To thank them for taking the time to make meal suggestions even sharing which entrees *they* liked in particular. They were always around, all omniscient, watching you from afar with a quiet, all-knowing and unselfishly caring agenda.

Wait! Did you just hear angels singing? Was there a sweet-smelling, gentle breeze that wafted past as your devoted server drifted quietly by? This uber waiter or waitress gave you the feeling that they were in that restaurant for one reason and one reason only. To wait hand and foot on you. Nirvana, wasn't it? Never wanted it to end, did you?

Now flash forward to that gum-chomping, annoying, non-caring piece of human excrement who not only took 30 minutes to bring a glass of water to your table, but he or she acted like it was their first day on planet Earth and that they were completely unimpressed by anyone or anything around them, including you.

You couldn't wait for the bill to come so you could give them a piece of your mind. Or maybe you'd stiff them. Or better yet, give them a piece of your mind and *then* stiff them. Yeah. That's it. You'll never darken the doorstep of that horrible restaurant again, never mind telling all your friends to avoid the place. F*ck them and that stupid, lazy, unenthusiastic, pretty-sure-they-were-on-something waiter/waitress. You'll show them.

Welcome to the journey you are about to embark upon. Hiring employees. If you think I was being overly-dramatic with the waiter/waitress comparison I just gave, think again.

Close your eyes for a minute and try to recollect either a wonderful customer service experience you had or a nightmare experience you've had. And we've all had both. How did that make you feel? With the positive experience, you find yourself wanting to patronize that business again. If the service was exceptional, you'll recommend them. Everyone has "a guy" they'd like their friends to use.

Now recollect your experience with say, a horrible hair stylist or uninterested checkout boy or a rude parking attendant. How did it make you feel?

Now think about your negative experience. You'll never go back, never use that person, never patronize that business or recommend them. And if the opportunity arises, you'll bash the crap out of them because you feel that you've been wronged. And frankly, if the service was bad, you have been.

Our employees are the ambassadors to our business. They are our "Walmart greeters." A lot of the time, your employees are the first point of contact with your business that the outside world has. And while you originally had been the first point of contact, as your business grows you find yourself doing different things and you just can't be on the customer front line any more. It happens. But that is the very reason why you need to think long and hard about who and why you hire.

A lot of companies make the mistake of hiring out of need and then rush into a hiring situation that may not be ideal due to desperation. As hard as it is to have an employee "hole" to fill, never hire in haste. Nine times out of ten, it will end up badly. Remember, it's a lot harder to fire than it is to hire.

When we first opened our doors and could afford to finally hire help, we did so by posting ads on Craigslist or by asking if anyone was interested on our personal Facebook pages. In the beginning, family and friends were happy to help out, but that was just a temporary solution.

I'm happy to report that now our hires are mostly referrals. We've learned to think out of the box when it comes to hiring. For example, our decorators are art students. We find that they're talented and creative and can easily make the jump from the medium they were schooled in to working with fondant.

Our bakers come from culinary backgrounds, some of them being hired because they were pastry school interns and we wanted to keep them on board. They knew us and we knew them. It was a seamless transition for them and our company. I *love* interns.

We have 20 employees now in Massachusetts, including our sales team at our Faneuil Hall location. That's a lot of employees considering we started with just the two of us.

When we hire, we take the usual suspects into consideration – availability, proximity to the shop, and experience. But the biggest thing I look for is what they actually say when I interview them.

I want to bring a happy and positive worker into the fold. If I hear any bashing about their last position, or a co-worker or boss, even a competitor of ours, I know they're not going to be the right fit with the rest of the team. And I do mean team.

We work as a cohesive unit. I don't tolerate employees who don't think of the others who are working with them. During their interview we stress the importance of teamwork, of helping a fellow employee out if they're having a hard day and are off their mark. It doesn't kill anyone to pick up some of the slack if someone else is struggling for any reason. Look, I'm one of the company owners and if I can bring out the trash, wash dishes or sweep the floor, so can everyone else. It's just that simple.

My employees work on an honor system. We trust that when they walk through the door they're at work, ready to work. I don't want to have to be a slave driver. I honestly don't have time for that. And I don't want to nag.

By setting very clear expectations in the beginning, everyone knows who does what and what's expected of them. So when expectations aren't met, it's easier to approach the subject because everyone is on the same page. Make sense? This allows me to run a place where people like coming to work, get along with each other, and get things done without having to be the warden.

As an owner, I feel that I also have a responsibility to my crew. I ask myself the following questions:

Am I available, approachable, and reasonable? My employees need to feel "safe" in their workplace. This means that there can be no gossiping, no playing favorites, and 100 per cent transparency.

We've had a ton of growth in a very short amount of time – 600 per cent in one year. Think about that! So I feel the need to keep everyone up to speed when it comes to changes in production, leadership, product, and scheduling. Nothing spreads like a cancer faster through a work place than supposition and comments made with little or no basis.

I also have found that by being willing to be open and honest with those I work with, they feel compelled to behave in the same manner. A negative company culture can hurt even the greatest of business plans and intentions. Rumors start, word gets out and then it's *really* hard to find great employees, because no one in their right mind wants to work in an environment like that.

One thing to keep in mind is how difficult a startup can be for some people. There are people who really need the security of knowing what to expect each and every day. The whole roller coaster ride that comes along with being a new business with rapid growth (did I mention 600 per cent in one year?) can be unnerving for some. It's imperative to keep good, strong lines of communication open with your crew. Allow them to voice concerns and even question the path the company is on. Remember, while it is your business and you do have the ultimate say, this is also someone else's livelihood. That's not something to be taken lightly or for granted.

Always remember to recognize milestones like birthdays and anniversaries. Give credit where credit is due. If one of your customers remarks on how an employee did a great job for them, then for the love of God tell that employee! Everyone under the sun needs to be thanked and wants to be appreciated. By recognizing a job well done you're not only giving much-warranted praise, but you're also showing everyone you're aware of what's going on and that you're watching.

Team morale is important. I like to buy lunch every now and again for no reason other than to say "thank you." Maybe it's a really hot day and everyone would love a cold iced coffee or iced tea. Do it. In the grand scheme of your business, it's not a lot of money spent, but it's money that is *well* spent.

Recognize the skill set your employees show and put them in a position to succeed. If "Mary" was hired to bake, but has a flair for decorating, then maybe "Mary" needs to go where she'll be happy and productive. There have been a few instances where we've hired people for one position and moved them into another. It may be because a position was no longer needed, but we've wanted to keep this great employee on. Or maybe the employee works better alone. Maybe he or she thrives in a team environment. Take the time to watch and see what fits best.

Ask how your employees are. Be interested in their lives. You don't need to become their best friends, but showing interest makes people feel valued and that you care. In turn, they'll want to work as hard as they can for you. "Please," "thank you," and "I'm sorry" go an awfully long way. These are words that should be used regardless of position or business stature. People are people and should be treated as such.

Our employees have made some excellent suggestions in regards to production, flavor profiles, even ideas for charitable donations. I like to have quarterly team meetings where we go through the company's health and current path and ask for any suggestions in regards to what we're doing and how we can make things easier and more efficient. In essence, how to make things better for everyone.

There's a strong sense of personal value that people feel when their ideas are listened to. Not every idea will work, but some are really great. Everyone wants to feel important and needed. Remember, these are the people who are handling your baby. Your business.

The recipe that works for hiring and team building is this:

1) What type of business are you building?

Just like the ingredients for a cake are different than a recipe for a loaf of bread, you need to know who works best for your business. Don't just throw anyone into the mix. Remember, it's easier to hire than fire. Source out the best employees you can and your recipe will be a hit.

2) Give your business hires the time to "rise" to the occasion.

In the beginning you may hire someone for one position, but find that they are better suited for another. By allowing your hires the opportunity to settle in and show you what they can do, you'll be able to shift people around and give them the opportunity to shine. It takes a lot of time and patience, but growing your team is like waiting for bread dough to proof. Let it take the time it needs to rise and then you're ready to get bakin'!

We're in a bit of a unique position, as this is a real family business. I work with my daughter and my husband. My ten-year-old niece developed a product. Think about that. That alone presents a number of situations that invariably arise.

Dani Had a Wingman

Nora Weiss and Dani have been friends for many years. When the opportunity came to have Nora join the Wicked Good family, everyone was delighted, especially Dani.

Nora shared her thoughts about joining the Wicked Good Cupcake family. "I was anxiety-ridden and I actually remember the moment that Dani and I discussed coming to WGC. It was a day I was incredibly angry with myself. Here I was – a recent college grad with a great job - and I was miserable. I walked around utterly convinced I was on the verge of being fired at any moment. Every day I told myself, 'You don't deserve this job,'" said Nora.

"You think that version of me is a mess? Oh boy – you should have seen me before when I was applying to job after job. It's a pretty typical millennial post-grad situation: 56 cover letters sat in rigor mortis in my "sent" folder, totally unanswered. My top searches in Google after graduation were 'how to get a job,' 'resume examples,' and 'do homeless shelters accept post-grads?'

"Even when I finally did land that job, I kept researching the statistics on people under 30 getting fired. I constantly told myself I was living on borrowed time.

"Entering college in 2008 and graduating in 2012, I was one of the many children of the American recession. Hell – I made sure to only invite family to my graduation party. Their awesome "Congrats Grad" cards were filled with cash that paid my rent that month. Right then, I was convinced debt would rule my life and I would never be a success."

Nora explained, "So there I was, rocking back and forth Sunday night through Friday, trying to exceed my own expectations. There were nights I cried myself to sleep because I was convinced the next day would be my last. I gained weight because I spent more time working at home after work than going to the gym. Even friends stopped inviting me out because I glued myself to my laptop, never looking away. But I told myself, 'This is your life now. This is how adults live and you need to pay rent.'

"My only saving grace was my evening phone calls to Dani. I would ring her on my way to the T. [Boston's infamous underground] and we would both bitch about our days. She would ramble on about prepping to grow her business and how her new retail store didn't have a manager; I would roll my eyes about how – yet again – I had let my teammates at work down. Dani and I were both coming from incredibly different places, but it was nice to see we still had common ground," said Nora.

"Dani never did the college thing, so it bugged me that she had a business to call her own at the mere age of 23 [at the time]. To me, Dani had struck gold: she wasn't in debt, she was her own boss, and she was ultimately doing something she was confident in.

"Yet to Dani, I was having the time of my life. I got to party my way through college, meet tons of great people, and now I was spending my time bar-hopping on the weekends. It's just funny what we allow other people to see of ourselves, and vice versa.

"Then came that day when I finally just cracked. I was standing outside my office; it was March and I'm on the phone with Dani. She barely managed to say hello when I blurted out, 'I'm doing it. I'm going to quit and work for you,'" exclaimed Nora.

"Yup, I was quitting my nine-to-five corporate job to work retail.

"This was an incredibly terrifying moment for me. It was tough to find the 'real job' in the first place and walking away with no guarantee I would ever find another 'real job' in the future was terrifying. It was like someone told me to jump off a building and maybe land on a sturdy mattress below… 'maybe' being the key word. Obviously, I would be taking a dramatic pay cut, and sacrificing my nights and weekends. Anyone who found out what I was doing looked at me like I had nine heads.

"My first real day in the mix was our opening in Faneuil Hall, about a week after Wicked Good Cupcakes first appearance on *Shark Tank*. Boston's Faneuil Hall is one of the top 10 most-visited places in the world. That's a lot of people!

"I had to close up that night. Scott was gracious enough to come in and, while rolling his eyes at the miscounting in the register, trained me to close … once. That's when Tracey, Dani, and Scott said, 'OK, this is yours now.'

"While those three were building an e-commerce empire, I managed the brick-and-mortar setup. This meant I had to create employee policies, hire people and then train them, all while learning the product and policies myself. Despite this stress, I always had Dani, Tracey, and Scott's best interests in mind. I didn't shy away. I wanted to take on challenges with gumption and, mostly, I wanted to suffocate my fear," said Nora. She has suffocated her fears and gone on to become an important member of the WGC family.

Mi Famiglia ... Works for Me, but What About You?

Ah. Family values. The family tree. A family that plays together stays together ...

It's interesting that when Dani and I started our "business," we didn't have a business in mind, per se. We were just enjoying doing something together. And I'll say that after a few rough patches, that's still the general consensus. We're a family that enjoys working and being together.

But this places us in a bit of a unique position, as this is a true "family business." I work with my daughter and my husband. Think about that. That alone presents a number of situations that invariably arise. In the beginning, not every day was enjoyable or easy. I was probably the biggest problem because I could not stop being "Mom."

I found myself being much harder on Dani than I was on anyone else. There was that classic power play between mother and child happening. In looking back, I have to say that she was a saint. I know I was tough. We have two very different personalities: me being the overly and tightly-wound Type A nutball and her being the laid-back, "I'll get to it when I can" sort.

Top all of that off with her moving back home. Not only were we at work six days a week, 15 hours a day, but we lived together as well. It was difficult for me and I can only imagine how incredibly hard it was for her.

It wasn't until a good year later, after we had been on *Shark Tank* and needed to define our roles, did we finally settle into a proper work relationship. For me, being able to watch her grow into her position, learn the ropes quickly, and be able to run a multi-million dollar business was the eye-opener.

I respected her and her vision for what she felt needed to be done for the health of the company, as well as the day-to-day operations of the shop.

I remember watching and listening to her one day and thinking, "Man, she's come *so* far!" I further thought, "Wow. She really knows her sh*t." Nowadays, it's kind of funny, because she'll assign me tasks to do when I'm at the shop. I love it. I love experiencing her confidence and leadership. I find great joy in seeing the business woman she has become. It's been one of the many joys and blessings I've come to enjoy throughout this crazy ride we're on.

But what if Dani's personality had been different? What if she were Type A like me? That's a scary thought. I'm not sure we'd both still be around. We might have killed one another.

This is a very important point to consider if you are toying with the idea of working with family. I want you to think long and hard about the personalities that will be coming together in the name of family business. Don't get me wrong; working with family can be one of life's greatest joys, never mind the legacy you'll create and eventually leave behind. But there's also a crazy power balance that cannot be ignored.

Dani and I have shared experiences that most moms and daughters don't have the opportunity to share. We know each other so well it's almost scary. When one of us walks through the door in the morning, before we've had a chance to exchange greetings, we know each other's moods. But this intimate knowledge of one another can also be very helpful. Situations can be much more easily diffused or avoided all together if one is keenly in tune with a business partner.

There's a definite dance that occurs when two people know one another so well. One can pick up the other's slack and work can become seamless. There's a level of trust that's there because of the family ties you share. But advantages can be taken, too. And it's awfully hard to discipline or even fire a family member even though it may be 100 per cent warranted.

Strong boundaries are a must. We have a mantra that goes "When we're at work, we work. And when we leave, we go home. Work stays at work." The point is to try and leave work and all of the minutiae at the place of business. Of course, this doesn't always happen, especially when the business is your family's. But by striving to keep work arguments out of the homestead, it makes for a much healthier and happier life for everyone. Work is work and home is home.

I also have the distinct pleasure of working with my spouse. Scott joined Wicked Good in January of 2014. This was a very good thing. Not only because the business was getting too big for Dani and me, but because he was working on it anyway during every free waking moment he had available. Poor guy. It was a lot.

I think for him, by placing the stake in the ground and leaving a very lucrative position, it made the business really *real*. No more safety net. It was do or die. It was exhilarating and frightening all at once and in order for us to climb to the next level it needed to be done.

For the most part, Scott and I are able to work and live together in relative harmony. We're both Type As, but with different strengths. It's important to recognize each other's strengths and to try not to infringe on someone's "thing." We work hard to always maintain a level of respect and professionalism. We speak to one another like we speak to our employees, and by that I mean not dragging any personal references or sh*t into a lively debate we might be having. Of course, this is way easier said than done. I've had many a drive home where I have had to remind myself just exactly why I married him and why I love him. It's tough sometimes. I won't lie. And I'm sure he feels the same. Only God knows how many times I've almost ended up with a pillow over my face while peacefully sleeping.

Fortunately, we are both crazy for the business (and each other) so the fact that we talk about nothing else is okay. For us. This can be hard for some couples and understandably so. My take on this is it's probably easier for couples working in the same business than it is for couples who have separate work lives.

I can only imagine the stress that must exist when one partner is investing all of their waking time and money into a "dream" while the other is left to support everything else. There needs to be a very clear set of boundaries and a willingness to give and take or the relationship won't last. There are a myriad of sacrifices – financial and personal – that are made by the entrepreneur and for the most part that's fine for them. After all, it's their passion and life. That's the road they've chosen. But that being said, the entrepreneur needs to make a conscious effort to understand that the partner in the equation didn't necessarily choose this way of life and may, from time to time, feel frustrated, ignored, and scared.

If you're starting to build a business, try and involve your significant other whenever and wherever you can. Draw lines in the sand concerning how much will be spent and where the buck will stop. Leave no gray areas, because this is where miscommunications will happen and fights will ensue. Remember that you may have decided to dedicate yourself to your new company, but you dedicated yourself to someone else first.

And if you're the lucky spouse or partner of an entrepreneur (entrepreneurs are so much fun) you need to be reasonable and give, too. You must make your needs and expectations known from the beginning. Don't play the nagging martyr. You both can survive this crazy ride if you both respect one another and support each other's needs. Communication and support are key!

Owning a Business is not All Glamorous

After three years in business, we took our first vacation. We went to Paris for two weeks. Normally, I would have been in Parisian heaven, but for some reason I was incredibly homesick by the third day in. All I wanted to do was go home and jump back into work. Thankfully, my crazy husband felt the same. So on day number seven, we headed back home. If I had been married to someone else, that could have been World War III. That's why knowing your business partner/family member's personalities comes into play. It's the type of intimacy that comes from eating, working, and sleeping side-by-side each and every day. It has its moments, but truth be told, I wouldn't have it any other way. He's the love of my life and that's what I think about at the end and beginning of each day.

Since airing on *Shark Tank,* we've added another family member to the staff. My 10-year-old niece Samantha. She worked with me to launch a product, Samantha's Cookie Jars, which features chocolate-dipped and decorated cookies just like the ones she and I made at holiday time for friends and family.

I can't put into words just how amazing it has been to see this business blossom and grow with friends and family. The sky's the limit for us. We're blessed and grateful. We know that we have something very special that precious few get to share with their own family members.

I'm so looking forward to more and more family joining the ranks. Wicked Good Cupcakes has been a dream come true and an amazing way to spend family time together.

My recipe for making a family business work is simply to:

1) Hold each other to the same standards you would if they were a non-family employee.

2) Create and maintain boundaries. No family "stuff" in the work place. Ever.

3) Make the expectations for everyone known. Define who does what and stick to it.

4) Communication and no gray areas help deflect any miscommunications.

5) Let it go. At the end of the day you are a family. Leave work behind and go home, to home.

Are You Social? Social Media Stuff

Starting a business in this day and age is certainly different than it was 20 years ago.

Before social media, getting the word out that you were "Open for Business" was much more of a challenge than it is now. Social media can be an amazing and *free* way to share with the world what you do and how to reach you. Did I mention this is free?

Gone are the days of real estate ads in the Sunday paper. Everything is online. The good news is, all of this information is available 24 hours a day, 365 days a year. I consider our online presence our biggest storefront. People can shop when they want, any time of day and any day of the year. But with all of the good also comes the bad.

Your website must be reliable. You need to comply with all state and federal regulations. Internet security should be your number one priority.

Your website must be relevant. It should be evolving and changing. You need fresh content, not only for your customers who visit, but for SEO rankings as well. Nothing drives your SEO up faster than content, online (articles, video, TV, etc.) as well as what's on your website. Don't fall for the empty promises from companies promising to zip your business up to the top in SEO rankings. Pay per click, all of the promises are a waste of money and time. Your climb up the SEO ranking will be slow but steady (think "The Flywheel" concept).

"The Flywheel" is a very useful analogy for implementing business strategy, created by Jim Collins. It describes how driving a new strategy is like getting a huge flywheel into motion. Initially, there is no movement – many people think that the strategy is absurd – it is almost impossible to imagine the flywheel at speed. With great exertion of will, the CEO is able to deliver some results that get the flywheel moving. They appear small and trivial initially, but create the credibility to move to more ambitious results. As more and more results accumulate, more and more people throw their weight behind the wheel and the momentum of the flywheel builds and builds.

Popularity of your site, keywords, blogs, other sites referencing and linking to you, basic tagging (alt tags, title tags) all work.

It's easy to become lazy about it. But I'm here to tell you don't be. There should always be a reason for people to come and check you out. FOMO (the fear of missing out) on something is a powerful call to action. Don't disappoint by having old, irrelevant content.

Another big question? Are you mobile friendly? More and more people now shop online using their phones. If your website isn't responsive, remedy that. Like yesterday. Otherwise you are losing money in sales!

The social media platforms that you use also help drive up your SEO as well as guiding people to your website.

Facebook, Twitter, Instagram, LinkedIn, Pinterest … social media is everywhere and a wonderful platform you can utilize to promote your business, your brand, even yourself. But knowing how to use it is the tricky part.

I love looking at photos of beautiful things. These images inspire and excite. Clearly, I can't be the only one, as social media appears to be everybody's favorite pastime. And while I lament the bygone days of handwritten thank-yous (along with the ability to not be quite so reachable), I've subscribed to the fact that if I can't beat it, I need to join it. After all, your future customers are all on board, so you need to be as well.

Wicked Good currently utilizes the following platforms: Twitter, Facebook, Instagram (although not as much as I should), LinkedIn, and Pinterest. We've made some Vine videos and are working on a "Wicked Good TV" channel for YouTube. Quite honestly, I could spend a large percentage of my day just trying to keep up with these fast-paced outlets. And I do. Consistency and frequency of posts/images and tweets grab attention. Just be careful not to overdo it. Empty content is worse than none.

In a nutshell, we use Twitter for business-related announcements that are timely and interesting to the general public. We do intersperse a few tweets about product, but we don't overdo it. I will readily admit I am struggling to find out the secret to gaining traction on the tweetosphere, but that's my struggle to figure out and hopefully not yours.

We do use Facebook, Pinterest, and Instagram more to showcase finished product, as we have a very visual commodity. There's nothing more impressive than a beautifully decorated cake. Instagram gives you the option to change the lighting and mood if you will, making your product look wonderful. I love looking at great food shots on Instagram.

Facebook has an older demographic than Instagram. And although it's one of my least-favorite platforms, I know we need to have a presence there. Learn where your current customers hang and where your up-and-coming future customers gather. Try to have an appropriate presence on both.

One of the interesting/borderline annoying parts of Facebook is the reviews section. For a long time, we allowed people to leave reviews on our business page. But once we were on television, everything changed. Facebook got ugly. People started to say nasty things about Dani and me. People who didn't even know us were commenting on our intelligence, our looks ... everything. Competitors who had never even ordered from us (you better believe we can track and find all of this info out) were writing scathing reviews even though they never, ever bought a thing!

People who had made mistakes in their orders, such as an incorrect address, or who had picked a wrong shipping date, used social media as blackmail to get us to reship or refund – even when the problem was clearly not our fault. Threats of "if you don't, I'll go all over social media and bad-mouth you" were uttered more than once.

The final straw for us as a company came when a woman placed a large order and had it shipped to a clubhouse in the development where she lived somewhere in the Midwest. Long story short, the folks working at the clubhouse received her package and ate it! When she went to pick it up, they told her that they ate everything and to call Wicked Good to see what we'd do.

We reshipped (to her house) a new order. In the meantime, I tried for three days to reach the clubhouse manager to see if we could work something out. With the reship this was now a $200-plus incident.

On day four I finally reached the manager, who immediately lit into me. She denied knowing that the package wasn't theirs and told me because I was on *Shark Tank* I could afford to pay for the new order.

After we hung up, she went onto our Facebook page and reviewed us. She wrote her order was late, that the product was inedible, and that I personally screamed at her.

That was it for me. I disabled the review section and any comments we now receive are private. Let me tell you, I sleep much better at night since having pulled the plug.

When someone has it out for you, right or wrong, you are never, ever, ever going to win a fight on social media, so don't even try. If someone has a question or comment for us, we acknowledge the problem and direct them to customer service. End of story. And let me tell you that most of the time these people never even follow through. The internet has given certain people a type of anonymous power that can be used in the most irresponsible of manners. And we're not the only ones to have experienced such vile abuse. *Every* business I know has had some form of complaint, rant, out-and-out bitchfest posted on their social media. And while for the life of me I cannot understand why someone would want to be so hurtful, it just happens.

Dani shared Jimmy Kimmel's "Mean Tweets" with me one day and I finally got it. People just love to hate on others, especially if someone has achieved some level of success. It's inevitable.

So now, as a means to get ahead of any sort of social media feeding frenzy, we send automated feedback forms out to our customers. A week after an order has arrived, a customer feedback form is automatically generated and e-mailed to that customer. This serves two purposes:

1. First, it gets us ahead of anyone who may have had an issue, like a shipment arriving late, and helps head off any potential social media bashing. The customers are always (pleasantly) surprised when we follow up immediately with a call. Most tell us that they filled out the form, but never expected to hear back. We then go a step further and reship. Our customers mean the world to us and by listening to them we are able to put our money where our mouth is.

2. Second, this type of communication can alert us to any sort of trend. If there's a problem, say with a particular flavor of cake and we see the same recurring complaint, we can head off the trend and fix the problem before it becomes widescale. These feedback forms helped us to identify a problem with one of our contract bakeries. The quality of the vanilla cake had degraded and we were able to approach the owner. Unfortunately for him, he didn't care and we were able to fire him due to his lack of concern for our product.

A tool such as a feedback form is key to keeping customers as happy as they should be and for finding and correcting problems before they become too big to control.

Be vigilant and watch your Facebook page and your Twitter feed so you can address any concerns before they turn ugly!

LinkedIn is our go-to guide to find the people we want to get in front of. For example, I will log onto LinkedIn and search an industry I feel is a good fit and for the appropriate people to reach out to.

I write an introduction email that I will cut and paste into several e-mails that I will send to the proper people in each particular company.

I make sure to address each recipient by name and I always offer to send samples for them to try, because I know that nine times out of 10 if someone tries our jars, they invariably end up using them. I honestly don't utilize LinkedIn for anything else. I think of it as my online address book.

One of the best pieces of advice I will impart upon you is this. When using your social media, you need to know when it's time to stop selling. Yup. That's right. Cool it with the hard sell. Think about how you feel. Do you like being constantly nagged and prodded to buy? It's kind of a turnoff, isn't it?

To be a real success with your social media you need to stop harassing your customers and followers. Instead of selling, why not offer them something in return, like a fun recipe? Or how about a link to an article that relates to your industry and is unique and interesting? Have a customer give-away, where you do something for the people who have helped build your business. Remember, it's not always all about you. You'll experience a better give-and-take with your customers when you ask them questions and empower them by inviting them to respond. Just be sure to monitor your online dialogue, as it can sometimes take a negative turn. Nobody needs or wants that.

My last bit of advice on this subject is this…Your business accounts are just that. Business accounts. Please don't climb on your soap box and start spouting off about religion, politics, and other competitors. *Never* bad-mouth another competitor! It seems like that should be common sense, but I've seen some ugly dialogue out there and it's just not cool.

Social media is a fun and *free* way to reach the masses. Take the time to read your posts or tweets twice before putting them out there. Check them once for grammar and spelling and a second time for content. Once you hit that button, you have launched your words into cyberspace and they aren't always easy to retract. Think before you tweet/post! And *no* drunk tweeting!

It is in Giving That We Receive

Remember how we talked about a mission statement? And how it defined your business and its core values? Another defining proposition for your business is its charitable obligation to the world around us.

Some things to ponder: does your business participate in any sort of charitable acts? Do you support a local charitable organization? A national one? Do you or your employees volunteer anywhere? Do you ever donate food, product, or money? What is your business's platform on the fine art of giving back?

I have to say, it used to really bother me to ask an organization to which I was donating to give us some love back, whether it was in the form of a mention on social media or in an event program. But boys and girls, I have quickly learned that is the relationship that exists between nonprofits and the companies donating to them. And it is a perfectly accepted (and expected) part of the dance.

When Dani and I started, we had an event that we would donate to each holiday. We provided cupcakes for the annual Massachusetts Society for Prevention of Cruelty to Animals tree lighting held in Boston. The MSPCA was an organization that we loved. After all, with six dogs between the three of us, it seemed like a perfect fit. And it was.

For the past three years, we ran a charitable event called "A Taste of Home." This was the simple brainchild of one of our decorators who loved watching Dani working with our troops' families here at home.

The idea is quite simple. On Veterans Day, we announce that our customers have the ability to pledge a cupcake jar for a reduced cost that will be shipped to a base overseas in Afghanistan or Iraq. Our customers are encouraged to write a personal message to the troops. We then enlist the help of grade school children across the nation to draw some holiday cards for us.

We pick a day in early December to invite the public to join us in what has been named our "Card Signing Event." Thousands of cards are signed and shipped mid-December along with the thousands of cupcake jars that have been pledged.

You would be so humbled if you could read the e-mails and cards we receive from the troops after they have received their surprise holiday treat. We have pictures and notes that we save and look at as a constant reminder that without our brave men and women, we would not have the freedom to be female business owners. Our "A Taste of Home" campaign is by far our favorite charitable event every year.

We've immersed ourselves in our community, which was the town of Cohasset, Massachusetts, and the South Shore. We took cupcakes left at the end of the day and dropped them off at local businesses, the town fire department, a women and children's shelter – anywhere we knew they'd be appreciated. We called it "Cupcake Bombing." In reality, we were executing our mission statement. This yummy surprise at the end of the day meant a lot to those we visited and no doubt helped build a strong community bond.

We involved ourselves with local school events, but that eventually became too much as surrounding communities began to ask for our help.

After our appearance on *Shark Tank*, the ante was just that much higher. On average now we must receive 8-12 requests for donations a day! Yes! A day. Naturally, we simply can't give to everyone. We'd be broke. We all sat down and decided which organizations we felt a connection to, as well as which of them were a good source of synergy for us.

To this day, I hate to say no. It troubles me that we can't help out each and every cause. But the reality is that we can't. So I try to make myself feel better by reminding myself that we are helping *someone*.

You may want to tailor which events you participate in based on the age group, socio-economic status, and region of the event. Yes, you are donating, but this is also Marketing 101, so make sure you're reaching an audience who will be motivated to check your business out and then ultimately buy from you. If you sell cake, working with the Diabetes Foundation may not be your dream match *unless* it's a cause near and dear to you. Then by all means have at it!

Make sure that the people who are attending an event know how to reach you. Try to get an ad in a program, your business name on a sign, and for goodness' sake bring business cards.

It's so important in this day and age that you have a presence in the big, wide world of giving. You're building relationships, creating good will, and spreading your reputation among potential customers. And at the end of the day, it just feels so good to be a part of something greater than you and your tiny world.

I Think Your Product Sucks.
But Don't Take it Personally

We all dread them. And yet there's no avoiding them. I'm talking about the inevitable customer complaint.

When we first opened our doors to the Cohasset shop, I was obsessed – obsessed with how the cupcakes lined up in the case, how the fondant flowers had to alternate in patterns on the tray. I felt a surge of pride with each beautiful tray that was placed inside the case each day.

And then it happened. The public entered our shop.

Now don't get me wrong. We had rave reviews, lines out the door, and tons of orders, but in looking back I was such a Pollyanna and felt like if I personally touched each and every cake, treated them like tiny children and made them look their best, no bad words would ever be uttered.

Wrong.

It started with the question, "Is that all you've got?" I would look quizzically at the customer leaning into (and smudging) the case. Was I missing something? We had ten different flavors in the case. What could they possibly be looking for? "Um, yes," was my go-to response. The customer would scan the case one more time and then order a vanilla cupcake with vanilla frosting. "Really?" I'd think *okay, maybe we need more variety*.

So now I added two more flavors each day. A dozen flavors. And *still* the question would be asked. "Is this all you got?" I'd crumble the bakery tissue in my hand, count to ten, and reply with a forced smile, "Yes." Now I follow up with "Is there anything in particular that you're looking for? We have chocolate/chocolate, chocolate with vanilla, chocolate with peanut butter, and hummingbird, which is cinnamon, pineapple, and banana. We have a lovely carrot cake with chocolate chips instead of raisins, we have vanilla/vanilla, vanilla with chocolate, red velvet, salted caramel, our samoa (people love that one), lemon, and coconut. Does anything speak to you?" The reply, "Yeah. Give me a vanilla, vanilla."

It actually became a joke between the decorators, Dani, and I when someone would come in, look at our 15 flavors and still ask what we had. I would usually walk out back and curse while everyone snickered.

And then one day it dawned on me. You just can't please everyone and you're a fool to even try. As long as our customer service was exceptional and the quality of our product was exceptional, then that was all we could do. Ultimately, I could have had 30 flavors in the case and someone would ask for more and then turn around and order a vanilla, vanilla. It was just that simple. Duh.

The other comment we got on occasion was, "They're too sweet." Hmm. I would scratch my head and think, well yeah. They're cupcakes and are made with sugar and chocolate. Of course they're sweet.

Again, we weren't going to please everyone. Given the business we were doing, enough people didn't think the cake was too sweet so I couldn't worry about it. You need to remember, especially with something like a food product, customer opinion is very subjective. Someone's idea of wicked spicy may be bland to another palate. If *every* person who bought something from us thought our product was too sweet, then there'd be a problem. But the comment was infrequent and people still bought our cupcakes anyway, so it became a non-issue.

After we aired on *Shark Tank,* we received tons of e-mails from people, most of whom were just trying to help, advising us on how to run our business. And while some of them were really sweet, others were pretty nasty. Unless there was an issue about a specific product, these horrible e-mails were never responded to. Why get into a pissing contest you will never win? These armchair entrepreneurs were just that, people. People who would never have the balls to put themselves out there, place themselves in an uncomfortable position and pull the trigger on their own business. Apparently for some it's easy to tell someone how they should run their business when you have nothing at stake.

Some of the more amusing feedback was:

"I bought your cupcake jars and when I tried to remove them from the jar with a knife they didn't look anything like a cupcake. You've ruined my dinner party." I guess she missed the part about them being ready to eat from the jar and the reason why we ship our jars with spoons. Sorry!

"The package arrived late and now my children are traumatized because their mother's gift was delayed." Umm. There was a tornado in the Midwest and UPS thought it the safer choice to ground their planes. Sorry!

"My neighbor's children ate our package. They did say the cupcakes were really good." Oops. Sorry!

"I live in Montreal, its 2:00 a.m. and I just smoked a bowl. I *need* your cupcakes right now!" Okay. We are working on shipping to Canada, so hang tight. Dude.

"I order your cupcakes once a month (you know, that time) and I'm convinced that they are the only thing that saves my husband's life. He thanks you for that." Some may file this under TMI. I thought it was brilliant.

And while these are just a few of the e-mails we have received that were really funny, some are not. Some are downright horrible.

You can criticize me, but my family and business are off-limits. Beware the Mama Bear!

Never, ever fall victim to mean-spirited, nasty people. Negativity is like a virus. Don't get sucked into that nonproductive world. It won't do you or your business any good. Learn to hit delete and let it go. I struggled to do this. I took everything to heart and it really hurt. Hearing that a competitor was going into the shop where I took my drum lessons and was bad-mouthing me hurt. Reading a tweet from some stranger telling me how stupid I was for taking a royalty deal hurt. Reading an email that called my daughter a skank because she had tattoos hurt. But for the sake of my mental health I had to ignore this crap and just move on. Clearly we had made an impression or they wouldn't have taken the time to do or say what they did. My brother Ted, an on-air personality, once told me "You're no one until they start talking about you." I think of that often. It's my go-to mantra when someone has shocked us (again) with some outlandish statement.

My husband always says it's tough to "lift the rocks" and see what's really underneath. It's hard to admit when a mistake has been made on our end, but it has to be done. It's also really difficult to take the necessary, critical look at your business. Face it, none of us are perfect and issues will arise. The good news (I guess) is that mistakes happen to everyone and every business. No one escapes unscathed.

Making Mistakes Pay

If you have the opportunity to go and listen to a successful entrepreneur, I encourage you to do so. I also encourage you to really listen as they tell their story. If they never mention any issues, problems, or f*ck ups, understand that they're not telling you the whole story. And that's really too bad. Because it's in our mistakes that we learn the lessons that make us bigger, stronger, and ultimately that well-oiled machine that we all strive to be.

Let me be the first to tell you we've f*cked up. More than once. And it absolutely *kills* me. I hate when an error occurs. It simply means someone was asleep at the wheel. Well, most of the time. There are third-party errors that occur (like delayed UPS deliveries) that truly are out of your hands. But at the end of the day it's still your business and you are the one who needs to take the fall. I find *pain* is a wonderful teacher.

I maintain that you need to experience three very distinct phases of pain when your company has made a mistake. The mistake has happened and it has sucked. Use it. *Learn* from it.

1) Feel it.

When you or an employee makes an error, big or small, you need to feel it. And I mean right to your very heart. That mistake should hurt you so much that you hear yourself utter the words, "That'll never happen again. That can never happen again." It's in feeling this pain that you learn your most valuable lessons. That awful experience that prevents you from ever doing what you or your business did again.

2) Fix it.

You may have something happen that is so upsetting that you can't even move. You can't blink, think, or act. I'm here to tell you, you must. And you must act fast. Save the finger-pointing and the blame game for later. Fix the damn problem! Especially if your customer is directly impacted.

We aired on *Shark Tank* at the end of April. We had tons of Mother's Day orders pouring in because of that segment. Our co-producer (at that time) had an issue in their kitchen that prevented 400 orders from shipping. That would have been bad enough, but this happened on a Wednesday and because they were afraid to, they didn't tell us until Friday afternoon! What!?

To make a long and ugly story short, I spent all day Saturday calling each and every customer to tell them that their order wasn't shipping, while Scott sat beside me refunding them. I'm sure I don't have to tell you how devastating this was for us. I was in tears most of the day. The majority of the customers were disappointed, but said that because we contacted them and refunded immediately that they would take a chance on us and order again. And then there were the ones who were (rightfully) really angry. Those were awful phone calls. And every single one of them hurt. But we had to put our fear and dread of making those calls aside so that our customers would know what was going on and that we were working hard to fix things.

So #1. Feel it. Yup we sure did. And #2 Fix it. We really tried.

3) Forget it.

Okay, for me this is by far the hardest part of a mistake to address. I cannot easily let things go. Just writing about that awful, awful Mother's Day still causes me to feel that pain. But I learned that once a problem was addressed and corrected I *had* to let it go. Hanging on to that sheer misery wasn't good for business and it definitely wasn't productive. So instead of cringing every time I thought about it, I used that horrific experience to get our systems in order, to make the necessary decisions that needed to be made, and then act upon those decisions to correct and then ensure that a mistake like that Mother's Day would never, ever happen again. You must move on and let this mistake go. Learn from it and then forget it happened.

Complaints, Negative Nellies, errors, and sh*t will just happen. It's all in how you handle these issues that will set you apart and define your business. We have had customers that will never come back to us. It hurts, but it happens. I'm proud to say that we've learned a lot in the past (short) three years and have a very high repeat business rate of 40 per cent and high marks on our customer feedback forms. But this success has come with a lot of lessons and the consequential pain.

Be brave and turn over those rocks. Listen to your customers and sift through the valid comments and complaints and toss aside the ones that don't make sense or apply.

Never get into a fight with your customer. You'll never win. You're not going to please everyone and everyone is not going to love you. And that's okay. To each his own.

Treasure the customers you do have. Especially the ones who are your staunchest supporters. Without them, there would be no business. We can learn a lot and teach a lot if everything and everyone is handled in a positive and respectful fashion.

A Little Bit of Luck

And so it would seem that we have had some luck on our side. But I can confidently say had we not worked hard and been ready for our opportunities, no amount of luck would have helped. You see, at the end of the day, we're responsible for making our own luck. And if we hadn't worked hard to put all of our systems into place, we may have had an epic fail after *Shark Tank* and no amount of luck can ever bring back an opportunity that was missed.

We needed to be ready to execute. And we were. That's not to say there weren't any hiccups. But we were as prepared as we knew how to be.

Work hard, be prepared, and luck will find you. I promise.

www.WickedGoodCupcakes.com

CHAPTER 11

LESSONS LEARNED

Failure Can Be Your Friend and Mentor

People have an inherent fear of failure. As one who has failed and messed up so many times, being afraid of failure is a really hard concept for me to grasp. I have been forced to make decisions that I *knew* were destined to fail, but the alternative was even worse.

The fact of the matter is as simple as this: if you have an idea that excites you and you believe it could be successful, unless what you are considering doing is going to cause you to lose your family, all your money, your home, or your life, then there is no reason not to take a chance. Being afraid that someone may laugh at your idea, or give you a hard time about not having as much free time as you used to (for them), then you have to pull yourself out of your security zone and take a chance.

For me, the thought of living with the nagging "What if…?" In the back of my mind for eternity is worse than any f*ck-up or mistake I could ever make. I never want to live with regret.

While attending Boston Conservatory, I had the opportunity to take a job at Opry Land. If I had seized that moment and gone, I never would have become pregnant and would have realized my dream of being a professional dancer. It's easy for me to say now that everything happened the way it should have and I do believe that. But the real reason I didn't take that job was because I was afraid. I was afraid to go and live in a different state by myself and that stopped me. So the question is simply this: Was I really destined to be a performer? Or did my real success need the time it took to find me? I'll never really know the answer to that. Or do I?

Why Fear is Healthy and Necessary

After having been in business with Wicked Good for two and a half years, I went on a short but very much-needed trip to Costa Rica. While there, I had a lot of opportunities to participate in some activities that normally don't present themselves to me in my everyday routine.

Unfortunately for me, and for my fear of heights, these sports were to be performed well above sea level.

The first full day there I rappelled down five different waterfalls, the highest being around 140'. As I stood (trembling) on the edge and peered over, I felt a moment of panic followed by the unnerving feeling that my legs were going to collapse.

My brain could compute that I was harnessed, tethered, and had two guides tending to my lines, but the pit of my stomach wasn't buying it.

Sadly for me, there was no turning back. I could opt to spend the rest of my days in the dense, steamy jungle, or I could trust that the people working with me were professionals and knew what they were doing.

After a minute more of contemplating death, I bit the bullet and jumped backwards over the edge.

That liberating feeling of fright, excitement, and accomplishment was exuberating. The next day I ziplined 550' (that's 50 stories, folks) and walked over swaying hanging bridges. I'm still respectful of heights and I'm not over my fear by any stretch, but I have to say I was proud of myself for facing that fear and taking the plunge (literally).

Business is no different. I live with a healthy amount of fear every day when it comes to Wicked Good. Not the debilitating fear that prevents one from screaming when a zombie comes running for them, but the type of fear that keeps you on your toes.

I fear that business will end. I fear that my creativity will dry up. I fear that business will slow down and I'll have to let employees go. I worry about the weather and deliveries. You name it. I worry about it. But rather than letting my fears paralyze me, I use them to make me work smarter, harder, and safer.

When we started our business, I worried that I would never be able to handle the workload. But I did. I worried that I couldn't keep inventory, make a schedule, or even get through a tough day. But I did. What if we didn't make any money? We did.

And the truth of the matter is, the more I feared, the more I taught myself about the very thing that scared me. Once you decide to go into business, you need to commit and jump off the edge.

Just like you can't rappel down a waterfall halfway, you can't start a business halfway either. You're either all in or you're not.

I guess the moral is this: fear is good. It keeps you sharp. It keeps you safe. Don't let fear keep you from doing the things you really want to do. Surround yourself with "guides" who can be trusted and have the knowledge about things you don't.

Starting a business is exhilarating and terrifying all at once. Once you start your descent into your business you can go as fast or as slow as you want. You're in control. Speed is not important. Having faith and facing your fear is. Strap on your harness, trust your guides, jump off that ledge, and enjoy the rush.

Congratulations! You've just conquered a fear that so many want to overcome and very few do.

You've started a business.

When you first set out to create a new business you'll find that downtime is hard to come by. Why, it's practically nonexistent. And that sucks because it's when we're most relaxed that new and creative ideas flow. When free time was a luxury for me, I made the most out of everyday activities that I found enjoyable and used that time to let my brain relax and let my mind unwind.

Taking a walk or a relaxing bath were two of the methods I used to help stimulate my creativity. The only caveat I will give here is that you need to have a notebook and pen nearby or your fabulous new ideas will go down the drain with the soap bubbles! Recharging oneself by whatever means is vital to not only your mental health, but the health and well-being of your business!

If You're Not Happy, Nobody is Happy

What brings you joy? What do you do for *you?* Is "me time" selfish or a necessity?

Picture this. 6:00 a.m. A mom jumps up out of bed and splashes water on her face.

She buzzes throughout the house from bedroom to bedroom waking children, all while picking up some random laundry items off of the floor.

The dogs go out, breakfast and lunches are made. She hops into a very quick shower, gets herself dressed, finds hubby's chronically missing keys, gets kids out the door, the dogs come back in and she's off to work. Whew. And if you're already familiar with this story, you already know it doesn't get any easier. A working mom's day doesn't end until she falls into bed at 10:00 p.m. that night.

I dare say, this is the life of a working mom. And working dads, for that matter.

I don't think it's a coincidence that we're all experiencing a crankier, ruder, and truly angrier world.

A huge percentage of people today just don't experience any down time. They don't allow themselves solitude, "me time" or feel the joy that comes from following a passion.

"But Tracey," you may ask, "haven't you always said work should be your passion?"

Yes. Yes I have. And it should. But there is a caveat in that at the end of the day it's still *work*. And I firmly believe to be successful at work, we need to allow our minds and souls the time to relax and breathe to recharge our creative batteries.

Recharge Your Batteries
Before You Run Out of Juice

Building a successful brand has been a crazy, exciting and completely gratifying ride, but there is a part of me, my soul perhaps, that needs to feel the joy and freedom that comes with enjoying a hobby, discovering something new, playing sports, reading a book, cooking, and even taking a much-needed nap. Without that, I don't think we would have enjoyed the success we have enjoyed.

So many of us are driven by the want and need to be successful – successful parents, business owners, employees. We're so caught up in this fast-paced ride that we've forgotten how to decompress. When business challenges arise, it is logical that we would put in more hours and work harder; however, if you want to achieve a higher level of success, this may actually be the wrong approach. The right answer may well be to take a step back, clear your mind, recharge your creative batteries, and then come back to the problem. It seems counter-intuitive, but it is a common mistake that business owners make that can be fatal.

I think many of us feel guilty indulging our soul's wants or needs. We feel compelled to keep driving ourselves (and unfortunately for some, our children as well). Burnout is a real danger here, physical as well as mental. It's no wonder families fall apart. How can anyone be happy and refreshed when they're constantly going, going, going?

I'm here to tell you it's okay to stop. I'm asking you to stop. Cut yourself some slack, sit down, close your eyes, and breathe. There. Now listen to me.

Allowing yourself to have a rest, to take up a hobby or to read a book, is not a luxury. It's a must. And if you feel that spending money on playing a round of golf, learning how to ride a horse, or going scuba diving isn't in the budget, know that there are many ways to enjoy "me time" without breaking the bank.

Schedule some time for yourself. Shut off your cell phone! (Or better yet, leave it behind.) Take a walk in a park, on the beach, or in the city. Try not to think about anything but the moment you are experiencing. Sit on a bench and people-watch. Close your eyes and take a deep breath in. Exhale out all of the stress you're holding inside. Then keep your mind quiet.

Lie in the grass and watch the clouds. Say a prayer of gratitude. Enjoy the feeling of peace and contentment that comes with allowing yourself the time just to be.

Understand with the reality of our lives you may not be able to escape every day. But two to three times a week is not unreasonable. You do have the time. The hardest part of this exercise is just doing it.

Write "me time" into your schedule if that helps. Do anything you can to insure success. It's really hard to leave the phone behind and walk out the door. But I can tell you that once you do, I guarantee you'll want to again and again.

Our lives are busy. It's simply the fast-paced world we live in. But by allowing yourself an escape, whatever form that is, you will help yourself to remain inspired, recharged, and happy. Some of my best ideas, speeches, and marketing ideas happen on walks or during relaxing baths. It makes total sense. When my mind is at rest, I'm more creative and ideas begin to flow. It just happens. (Helpful Tip: Keep a notebook handy so you don't lose those precious ideas!)

Every Day Can Be Your Fresh Start

January 1 is the start of a new year; however, every day of the year can be treated as your new year.

I love thinking of new beginnings, no matter what time of year it may be. It's a time to say goodbye…

It's a new year. Dare to dream. Dare to fail. Dare to be a success.

I love the New Year. It's a time to say goodbye to the past, reflect on the lessons we learned, enjoy the victories we accomplished, and happily greet the new and all its potential.

I'm often asked what resolutions I have made for myself and the answer is the same every year. None.

I don't believe in resolutions. I think people start off with great intent, only to be really disappointed when they fail. People often pick a resolution that has to do with modifying a bad habit or some other negative aspect about their life. Maybe they want to work out more, but hate the gym. Maybe weight loss is a goal, but they hate dieting. Or maybe they want to spend more time with family, but giving up precious free time has just been too hard or just plain inconvenient.

I'm a very positive person. I'm someone who dreams big and works hard to achieve everything I feel like I can and I should. So the thought of starting off a new year, a clean slate if you will, with resolutions that force us to do something we haven't wanted to do or have dreaded doing the entire year before makes no sense. If we're starting out "anew," why not begin with positive aspirations? Dreams that you want to work towards, not resolutions that you dread working at.

Feel Your Way to Success

Take a second and humor me. Sit quietly with eyes closed and dare to dream a big dream. It may be as simple as a goal for work or maybe it's as big as a life-changing plan. Visualize yourself where you want to be, doing what you want to be doing. Feel the excitement build as you see the movie of your life in your mind's eye. See the faces of those who are a part of your grand plan. If it's a new product you're developing, "hold" that product in your hand. Really imagine what the labeling will look like. Picture it on a store shelf or on your website. Make this imagery as real as you can.

Open your eyes. Remember how you felt. Now take a journal, electronic tablet, a napkin, whatever you have handy, and start to write down how this dream of yours will begin to take shape. Keep this journal with you at all times. New ideas come at some of the most inconvenient times and you want to write everything down as soon as you think of it or you risk losing that brilliant thought forever.

Make your dream the last thing you think of as you drift off to sleep and the first thing you think about when you wake. Don't pressure yourself with arbitrary timelines. Dreams will take the time they're supposed to take.

You may find that you might have to take an unwanted break from your dream, as life has a way of taking over sometimes. That's okay. Remember each and every day will find you one step closer to achieving this goal. Enjoy the ride as you travel towards completion. Don't beat yourself up if it doesn't come together right away. Your biggest task is simply to believe in yourself and your dream.

Mistakes will happen. Failures and missteps will as well. Embrace them for what they are - lessons learned and just a part of the journey towards the end result. You'll never be able to really dream if you are afraid to fail. Everyone fails at some point in their lives. It's the dreamers who have the ability to pick themselves up and move on who succeed.

Our Wish for You From the WGC Family

And now you've read all about how a mother/daughter/husband/ stepdad team worked really hard and built a dream from the ground up. We're not brilliant, overly-educated, wealthy (yet) or finished growing, by any stretch.

Every day is a new day filled with ups and downs, challenges and successes, near-misses and home runs. All you have to do is decide if owning your very own business is for you. And honestly, if it's not, that's okay too. Not everyone is cut out to do what we do. That's for sure!

But if you love a challenge, you keep a notebook by your bed because you wake up with killer ideas, you don't mind eating take-out at 10:00 p.m. or getting up at the crack of dawn, living, breathing, and thinking about your passion, then by all means jump on in. The water's fine. You're an entrepreneur and it's time to start swimming!

My wish for you is that you discover a fantastic dream; one that's your own, and the patience needed, the willingness to stumble and fall, and the ability to find the grit within you to make this dream a reality for you and your loved ones. Peace.

www.WickedGoodCupcakes.com

SPEAKING

❖

Tracey Noonan and her daughter
Dani Vilagie are available to speak
at your next function.

Their honest humor about life and growing a
successful brand is sure to inspire, empower
and motivate your audiences.

To learn more, visit:
https://www.wickedgoodcupcakes.com/